Living Life
with
No Limits

Freed *by* God to Go Further *with* God

Delman L. Coates, Ph.D.

Renown Publishing
www.renownpublishing.com

Living Life with No Limits / Delman Coates
ISBN-13: 978-1-952602-45-0

DEDICATION

I dedicate this book to those who have added so much to my life. First of all, to my four children—Nathaniel, Joshua, Ava, and Leah—who are my heart and joy, and give my life meaning. I love each of you so much, and I hope that you will be inspired to pursue your dreams without limitations. I also dedicate this book to my parents—Lewis and Maxine Coates—who have given me the best parental and Christian nurture I could ask for, and to my sister—Treva—who has been a source of comfort and counsel during challenging times.

To the many friends and colleagues who inspire me, and to my amazing church family, Mt. Ennon Baptist Church in Clinton, Maryland—thank you for supporting me over the years of my tenure as pastor.

I am so thankful to have had so many networks of support and encouragement throughout my life as I have endeavored to be faithful to the assignment of God on my life.

CONTENTS

INTRODUCTION

Planting Trees

History is a seed planted in the past that produces fruit in the present. The landscape, the opportunities, and the needs of today are tied to the choices of those who came before us. Similarly, the choices you made in your past were seeds for the life you have today. The choices you make today will bear fruit for generations to come.

The tallest tree in the world is a coast redwood, measuring around 380 feet.[1] Yet between six hundred and eight hundred years ago, it started off as a humble seed.

Like trees, your life and circumstances grow from seeds that take root. And as with trees, those seeds had to be planted at some point.

Howard Thurman, theologian and mentor of Dr. King, told a story once about watching an old farmer working in a field one day.[2] The farmer was working with so much focus that he didn't notice him initially, until Howard spoke to him. Their conversation revealed that the old man was planting pecan trees.

Thurman was bewildered because he knew the trees were young and it could be a decade before they bore any fruit at all, but he learned from their conversation that this farmer was eighty-one years old. So Thurman asked the man, "Why did you not select larger trees so as to increase the possibility of your living to see them bear at least one cup of nuts?"

The man said, "All of my life I have eaten fruit from trees that I did not plant, [so] why should I not plant trees to bear fruit for those who may enjoy them long after I am gone? Besides, the man who plants because he will reap the harvest has no faith in life."

That farmer was more than a planter of crops—he was a nurturer of the generations to come.

This story shows why history is so valuable. When we review our history, we are reminded that we are the beneficiary of crops that prior generations planted. The stories of the past are worth telling, both because they remind us that we stand on the shoulders of others and because they can help ensure we don't repeat past missteps. Understanding errors of human judgment and action from the past can keep us from repeating the mistakes of bygone eras.

Charles C. Seifert expressed this point eloquently. He once said, "A race without knowledge of their past history is like a tree without roots."[3] Seifert was suggesting a truth that remains salient today: there is value in understanding the web of social, political, and economic events and developments that have transpired in the past. History is not a random collection of moments without relevance and significance, which can be ignored or forgotten without consequence. Those moments are the seeds and roots of our existence, individually and collectively. Past events shape us, move us, and enlighten us as we travel along our paths in life.

This truth is found in the Bible as well:

> *Give ear, O my people, to my teaching; incline your ears to the words of my mouth. I will open my mouth in a parable; I will utter dark sayings from of old, things that we have heard and known, that our ancestors have told us.*
> *—Psalm 78:1–3 NRSV*

The Israelites were trying to forge a sense of community in a society that sought to put them down, wipe them out, or push them away. They emerged in the midst of powerful empires like those of the Egyptians, Babylonians, and Persians. There was often pressure to blend in, by learning the history, culture, language, and religion of their oppressors—going along to get along for the sake of preserving some level of status, security, and wealth.

But the psalmist declared that God's people have a story to tell—a story of trial and triumph, of struggle and victory—and a sacred duty to tell it, even if doing so might rock the boat. Psalm 78:4–7 (NRSV) says:

> *We will not hide them from their children; we will tell to the coming generation the glorious deeds of the LORD, and his might, and the wonders that he has done.*
>
> *He established a decree in Jacob, and appointed a law in Israel, which he commanded our ancestors to teach to their children; that the next generation might know them, the children yet unborn, and rise up and tell them to their children, so that they should set their hope in God, and not forget the works of God, but keep his commandments.*

In other words, don't be ashamed to tell your story. Verses 1 to 3 convey a sense of urgency that certain stories told, customs learned, and traditions passed down from generation to generation must not be forgotten. To those who might say, "The past is behind us now. We're doing better now. Those in power now had nothing to do with the oppression of our people back then, so let's get over it," the psalmist said no. Israel had a story—a history—worth telling and retelling to future generations.

Like the Israelites, people of African descent have a story to tell. We are heirs of an amazing legacy, but our story, like Israel's, is marred by the stains of injustice. Ours is the story of a people brought to this nation to be used as property, and then treated as second-class citizens in a nation whose founding document, the Declaration of Independence, claimed that "all men were created equal and endowed by their creator with certain unalienable rights." This painful reality is further compounded by the fact that some of our own were complicit in the tragic events of slavery and Jim Crow.

But part of the problem is that we have been made to believe slavery is the seed of our history. As the great historian John Henrik Clarke declared, "Slavery is not the beginning of our history; it was a disruption of our history."[4] The knowledge that our past is nothing to be ashamed of—and that we have an amazing, awe-inspiring story to tell—is a crucial starting point.

History is powerful because it helps us stay in contact with the past as we move into the future. To paraphrase one philosopher, life is understood backwards and lived forwards.[5] If we don't tell our story, no one else will, and that understanding will be lost.

Our history reminds us of those who paved the way before us. Let's not move forward into the future without recognizing how our present blessings are a gift from those who toiled, labored, and struggled in the past. Present and future generations are the products of the prayers and protests of people who, whether we know their names or not, left legacies from which we all benefit. It reminds us that we are where we are today because of the doors they opened for us. We can pursue careers and education, vote, and live free because our predecessors fought, bled, and died.

As the psalmist explained to the Israelites, it was important to teach their children their people's history so "that they should not be like their ancestors, a stubborn and rebellious generation, a generation whose heart was not steadfast, whose spirit was not faithful to God" (Psalm 78:8 NRSV). It's no coincidence that the psalmist's recitation of history didn't try to sugarcoat the past. He mentioned their people's past stubbornness and rebellion, because the lessons of history include wrongs committed *by* the community, not just *against* the community.

Taking responsibility by learning from your mistakes is key for growth in your individual life, too. When people look at me now, they often assume I came from a lineage of well-spoken pastors. But in college, I was not the most articulate speaker—not even close! In fact, I ranked last among my freshman classmates.

In my freshman week at Morehouse College, I entered a competition in rhetoric, which was a big deal for students who aspired to be preachers. Within seven seconds of me delivering my sermon, the judges told me to sit down. Though initially stunned, I resisted any urge to tuck my tail and run. Instead, I stayed and watched the others, including upperclassmen who were gifted communicators.

Rather than let this experience tear me down or destroy me, I embraced it as an opportunity to grow and develop. That choice, to stay and persevere, was a seed that still affects my life today. From that humble seed, my life has grown in ways that would have astonished me as a college freshman. I certainly never thought I would pastor ten thousand people! My life is writing a history that will affect those who come after me.

As you dive into this book and learn more about how to live without limits—beyond the constraints the world might try to place on you, or that you might place on yourself—remember the seeds others have planted for you. It's time to nurture those seeds and reap a harvest, for yourself and for generations to come. At the end of each chapter, workbook sections will help you begin to process what it means for you personally to experience freedom from limitations in your life and relationships.

Remember your roots and the stories you've been handed. Tell those stories while planting seeds for the next generation and, like the coast redwood tree, embrace life without limits.

CHAPTER ONE

Want Better and Be Better

There once was a man whose life trajectory and choices, like those of many people, took him down a path he would later regret. His name was Zacchaeus. Luke 19 tells the story of this desperate man who met Jesus and turned his life around.

[Jesus] entered Jericho and was passing through it. A man was there named Zacchaeus; he was a chief tax collector and was rich. He was trying to see who Jesus was, but on account of the crowd he could not, because he was short in stature. So he ran ahead and climbed a sycamore tree to see him because he was going to pass that way. When Jesus came to the place, he looked up and said to him, "Zacchaeus, hurry and come down; for I must stay at your house today." So he hurried down and was happy to welcome him. All who saw it began to grumble and said, "He has gone to be the guest of one who is a sinner." Zacchaeus stood there and said to the Lord, "Look, half of my possessions, Lord, I will give to the poor; and if I have defrauded anyone of anything, I will pay back four times as much." Then Jesus said to him, "Today salvation has come to this

*house, because he too is a son of Abraham. For the Son of
Man came to seek out and to save the lost."*
—Luke 19:1–10 NRSV

The text describes Zacchaeus as a chief tax collector
and a very rich man. Tax collectors in antiquity were hated
by their fellow Jews and were considered sinners. They
were hated by the Jews because they worked for the op-
pressive Roman empire. They were considered sinners
because they were frequently dishonest and would often
collect extra money for themselves, since the Romans did
not pay them an actual wage.[6]

But in Luke 19, we find that Zacchaeus wanted to do
better. He wanted to return to the place where God desired
for him to be. How did he do it?

Chase Something Greater

First, he had to change what he was chasing. The sense
from the text is that all the upward mobility, material success, and financial gain Zacchaeus had accrued over the
course of his life was no longer enough to satisfy the hunger in his soul, his desire for something deeper and more
fulfilling. This longing had become so great that when he
heard Jesus was coming, he abandoned his dignity and ran
to meet Him.

Warren Wiersbe said, "In the East, it was unusual for a
man to run, especially a wealthy government official, yet
Zaccheus ran down the street like a little boy following a
parade."[7] Picture this wealthy man dropping all he had,
laying aside the formality and pretense that came with his

position, to run ahead of the crowd so he could see Jesus. Typically, only lower-class people, who lacked social mobility, would be seen running along Mediterranean roads trying to get a glimpse of wandering prophets, but Zacchaeus had reached a point where he realized it was time to change what he was chasing.

Consider the paradoxes in the text. Here was a man who was materially rich, chasing a man who was materially poor. Here was a man with some power, chasing a man who, in the eyes of the authorities, had none. But none of that mattered to him in the moment. Zacchaeus realized that after all he'd achieved, after obtaining wealth and status, there was still a void in his life—a void that could not be filled with worldly things. Jesus' presence symbolized a return to the moral center, the spiritual life that Zacchaeus had left behind when he chose another path.

And he wanted something different; something on the inside of Zacchaeus wanted to connect with Jesus. He was looking for something and someone greater. Whatever you call it, one of the richest men in town realized he had to respond to that inner impulse; he dropped what he was doing and changed what he was chasing. Until then, money and status had been everything. When Jesus came, he sensed he needed to meet with Him.

Elevate Your Life

In addition to changing what he was chasing, he had to elevate his lifestyle. The text says that this powerful government official not only ran after Jesus but climbed up a sycamore tree to get a good view, as well. Zacchaeus realized that in order to change his life, he had to elevate his life and rise above the crowd so he could see what he so desperately needed. This climbing of the sycamore tree was symbolic of our need to elevate how we are living so that we can see life the way God wants us to see it.

Many of us have been viewing life from ground level, but as long as we're living low, we are going to keep getting low outcomes. God says it's time to shift our perspective so we can view life, family, faith, and finances not on a worldly level, but from a spiritual vantage point.

Paul tells us in Colossians 3:1–3 (NRSV):

> So if you have been raised with Christ, seek the things that are above, where Christ is, seated at the right hand of God. Set your minds on things that are above, not on things that are on earth, for you have died, and your life is hidden with Christ in God.

The issue for Zacchaeus wasn't so much that the crowds were in his way. The main issue was his short stature. It seems to me that he had spent his life trying to make up for it by exerting power over people, to mask his insecurity. But he wanted to put the limitation of that insecurity behind him, and to overcome it, he had to climb the tree.

This is key, because pride could have kept him on the ground. Pride would have said, "Don't put your weakness or limitation on public display like that. Just man up and do the best you can." But I like Zacchaeus's decision here because he didn't let his pride get in the way of what he needed and who he needed to see. He didn't care about hiding his weakness any longer, or about what people thought or said about him. He needed something greater, and he knew that he was capable of being better than the man he had become. It was time to shake off his old labels and elevate what he was doing.

Don't Let Labels Define You

So many people are stuck spiritually because they are imprisoned by the results of their life choices, or the labels that society places on them: dropout, deadbeat, felon, addict, cheater, thief. But God says what you've done does not define who you are. You may have committed a crime, but you're more than a criminal. You may have lied, but you're more than a liar. You are more than your mistakes.

Labels are dangerous because whatever you label, you can limit; whatever you brand, you can restrict, and the reason some people want to label you is so they can disqualify you. But God is more interested in your future path than your past mistakes.

Take heed, child of God: don't ever let the devil equate who you are with what you have done.

Jesus stopped what He was doing and saw this person in the tree. He saw the man, not his profession. Rather than calling him by what he had done, He called him by name. And Jesus did the same thing for you and for me—regardless of what we have done, no matter how bad, no matter how unacceptable in the eyesight of others, He calls us by name. God doesn't define us by our past but calls us as He sees us: His children.

Can you imagine how Zacchaeus must have felt, sitting in that tree as Jesus was passing by? Jesus knew his name. I can just see him, touched to the heart, saying, "You know my name?"

And I guess that's why I like that song, "You Know My Name," by Tasha Cobbs Leonard.[8] When God knows your name, and not your mistakes, it gives you strength. While the public was talking about Zacchaeus and wondering how Jesus could go to the house of a tax collector, Jesus was more interested in him than in the labels associated with his past. That's why, if you're going to be a better person in this next season of your life, you're going to have to know your worth.

Know Your Worth

Don't let anything, or anyone, keep you from being the man of God or the woman of God that He wants you to be. It's like if you lost a hundred-dollar bill. It can be trampled in the mud, stepped on, even torn, but if it still has the serial numbers on it, it still has its value. It doesn't matter what you've done. It doesn't matter what you've been through. You still have value and an identity.

And while others might throw you away, God doesn't. I thank God that despite the stains on my moral resumé, He hasn't discarded me. I thank God that despite what I've done and what I've gone through, He kept me.

One of the reasons the writer highlighted those extremely negative aspects of Zacchaeus' life was to illustrate that there is no limitation when it comes to God's love. The apostle Paul put it this way:

> *For I am convinced that neither death, nor life, nor angels, nor rulers, nor things present, nor things to come, nor powers, nor height, nor depth, nor anything else in all creation, will be able to separate us from the love of God in Christ Jesus our Lord.*
> **—Romans 8:38–39** NRSV

I like this text because there's grace in it. If you realize there's something more to life, that you've deviated from your ethical center and moral foundation, you need to do the same as Zacchaeus. You need to change what you've been chasing. You've been chasing pleasure, but now you need to chase peace. You've been chasing money, but you need to chase the Master. You've been chasing earthly relationships, but you need to chase spirituality.

If you want to be better, do better, or have better, you must reach a point where what used to motivate you no longer does. Zack discovered that money had its limitations. It could buy him a house, but it couldn't buy him a home. It could buy him a donkey, but not a purposeful destination. It could buy him a bed, but it couldn't buy him rest. Everything he had accumulated was just masking the fact that he was missing something on the inside.

Changing from the Inside Out

I read about the embalming process of King Tutankhamun, better known as King Tut.[9] They placed a 24-pound solid gold portrait mask over the head and shoulders of the dead pharaoh. He was laid in a series of nested containers—three golden coffins, a granite sarcophagus, and four gilded wooden shrines—but underneath it all were dead

bones. It hit me after reading this that it does not matter
how much you adorn the outside if you're dead on the inside.

Zacchaeus—a rich, wealthy government official—ran
to see this no-name Jewish carpenter from a no-name
town in Galilee because he couldn't keep going through
life doing what he was doing. He had to change what he
was chasing.

He not only had to change what he was chasing, but he
also had to change how he was living. Only fools keep
doing the same things the same way expecting a different
outcome. If you keep doing what you're doing, you're going to keep getting what you're getting. There comes a
time in all our lives when the presence of God prompts us
to rise above the pain of our past, to rise above the hurt,
the letdown, and the disappointment, and to take things to
a new level. Only then will you see better. Zacchaeus discovered that as he moved closer to God, God moved
closer to him.

Although Zacchaeus' occupation as a tax collector was
such that he became defiled in the sight of people, and in
the sight of God, Jesus showed him compassion. It's sub-
tle, but it's significant. Zacchaeus had not been behaving
in a manner worthy of one made in God's image, but Jesus
respected his personhood even if He disagreed with his
practices. Zacchaeus' worth as a person, and his value as
a human being, were not nullified by the choices he had
made in his life. Despite all the extortion and defrauding,
Jesus did not define him by his deeds or his mistakes,
which demonstrates that our value is not determined by

what we have done, but by what we have the potential to become. As proof that Zacchaeus wanted better, he changed his behavior. In Luke 19:8 (NRSV), he said he would repay everyone he had defrauded "four times as much" and give half of what he had to the poor. That's because he realized that if you really want better, you have to be better. Real deliverance ought to result in repentance and transformation.

WORKBOOK

Chapter One Questions

Question: Sometimes it's only when we look back that we see the wrong turns we have taken. Can you identify any mistakes in the past that have negatively impacted your life? What could you have done differently?

_____

_____

_____

_____

_____

_____

_____

_____

_____

_____

Question: In what ways do you feel these mistakes define you in your eyes and in the eyes of other people? How does God define you?

_____

_____

_____

_____

_____

_____

_____

_____

_____

_____

_____

Question: If Jesus were coming to your community, how far would you go to have a personal encounter? What would you be prepared to change? In what ways would that affect your life and your lifestyle?

_____

_____

_____

_____

_____

_____

_____

_____

_____

_____

_____

Action: As a result of meeting Jesus, Zacchaeus was prepared to make enormous sacrifices to correct his mistakes. Make a list of the changes you need to make in your life to let go of the past and start over.

Chapter One Notes

_____

_____

_____

_____

_____

_____

_____

_____

_____

_____

_____

_____

_____

_____

_____

_____

_____

_____

_____

_____

_____

CHAPTER TWO

It's Already Paid For

I have a problem with over-packing. When I'm going places, I have a tendency to pack way more things than I really need. I'm a very organized person, and when I travel, I want to be prepared for any contingency. I make sure I have outfits and products for every occasion.

My kids and I were going on vacation; it was an adventure that they had been looking forward to for quite some time. Day one of the trip, we were scheduled to land, board a van from the airport to the resort, and then get a shuttle for the first adventure of the day, which included ziplining and a safari. We had about an hour and a half after the flight landed to make it to the shuttle. Just the right amount of time, I thought.

When we landed, however, we ran into a problem. The bus assigned to pick us up was not as large as I had anticipated, and the driver was unable to fit all our things on the bus. He kept showing me a paper from the resort, which said that each person should have one suitcase and one small carry-on bag. I had seen that, but I didn't think they meant it literally. And besides, it was an eight-day trip, and you have to be prepared for anything, right? To say the least, we had way more than one suitcase and one small carry-on per person.

Because we were in a remote area, there weren't other vehicles that could take us. We had to wait for him to make several trips from the airport to the resort, and by the time we got there and waited to check-in, we had missed the shuttle for the first activity of the day, which the kids had really wanted to do.

So there we were. Josh was angry, Nathan was indifferent on his headphones, and the girls were crying, because I had packed and it was my fault. There I was, stuck with four uncooperative kids, unable to move forward and enjoy the experience because I was carrying around too many bags.

It dawned on me later that because of the baggage they are carrying, people all around us are not enjoying life. Perhaps they're not carrying suitcases, but psychological bags, emotional bags, and spiritual bags are all weighing them down.

Weighed Down and Worn Out

One thing that makes my heart break is seeing people at the check-in counter of life unable to move forward and go to the next level because they are carrying around too many bags. They are weighed down, stuck, and frustrated by their heavy load acquired from past choices and decisions. Baggage like bitterness, resentment, and hurt from past relationships. Baggage from the trauma of their child-hood or spiritual baggage from a season of rebellion against God, parents, and authority.

Carrying excess baggage is heavy; it weighs you down; it costs you your peace, your joy, and your sense of ful-fillment; and when the trip is over, you realize you didn't even wear or use half of the stuff you packed. Truth is, many are stuck in life, broken by baggage they refuse to relinquish. They may be doing well: making nice money, living in a decent neighborhood, and immersed in all the trappings of worldly success. But on the inside, they feel a sense of restriction or limitation, almost like they can't go on because the stuff they are carrying is holding them down.

I'm talking to the father whose children rarely see you because you are too busy working—but in fact, you're compensating for the emotional scars you've carried since childhood, when your own father wasn't there for you.

I'm talking to the young adult still struggling with the residue of childhood neglect and abuse. The reason you don't trust people now is because the people you trusted as a child betrayed that trust and put their hands on you.

I'm talking to the woman still carrying around the scars of abuse, neglect, and abandonment from someone who didn't appreciate or recognize your value.

I'm talking to someone who has yet to open your heart to the possibility of loving again after a failed marriage or a broken relationship, because you're still carrying the pain of the breakup.

And I'm talking to someone carrying the baggage of church hurt, from bad experiences with those who claimed to represent Jesus Christ but ended up putting you down more than lifting you up.

Whatever burden is taking up space in your life, whatever baggage comes to distract you from purpose by reminding you of your past, I want you to know that God has a word for you: you can't let your baggage get the best of you.

No Going Back

That's what the writer of Hebrews tried to communicate to the believers who received his letter. Hebrews 8 reminds us of an ancient prophecy:

> *This is the covenant I will establish with the people of Israel after that time, declares the Lord. I will put my laws in their minds and write them on their hearts. I will be their God, and they will be my people. No longer will they teach their neighbor, or say to one another, "Know the Lord," because they will all know me, from the least of them to the greatest. For I will forgive their wickedness and will remember their sins no more.*
> **—Hebrews 8:10–12** NIV

The identity of the writer is unknown, but the content of this letter has inspired generations of believers with its emphasis on themes such as the great cloud of witnesses surrounding believers; standing firm in persecution; and faith, "the substance of things hoped for, the evidence of things not seen" (Hebrews 11:1 NKJV). The letter was written to a group of Christians who appear to have been in danger of renouncing their faith or drifting away from the truth. Some were already neglecting to meet with the community.[10]

The problem was that the former way of doing things left them spiritually unfulfilled, lifeless, and flat-out stuck. Nothing is worse than being in a place you don't want, with people you don't like, doing something you don't want to do. While they were contemplating going back to what was comfortable and familiar, God was doing a new thing before their very eyes. They just could not see it or understand it.

The past had become so powerful that it formed a spiritual yoke and created psychological baggage for them. The law, as they understood, it left them burdened by a form of perfectionist religion that couldn't be fulfilled no matter how hard they tried. But, according to the writer of Hebrews, God replaced the old system with a new one when Jesus died on the cross. The old system—with its hierarchies of chief priests and high priests, with its corrupted religious elite and its shame-inducing legalists, and requiring the constant sacrifice of lambs, goats, and doves—was replaced by a new order that only required the blood of One, once and for all. In order to receive the new promise, they had to be willing to give up the old.

To experience what God has for you, realize that you cannot keep holding on to what is behind you. You have to let go of all that baggage.

Toxic Baggage

The writer of Hebrews said that we should never allow what is familiar to hinder our freedom, because it encumbers not only us but also those connected with us. Your families, your households, your relationships, and your friendships can all suffer because of your baggage. In *Healing the Shame That Binds You*, John Bradshaw says, "Toxically shamed people tend to become more and more stagnant as life goes on. They live in a guarded, secretive and defensive way. They try to be more than human (perfect and controlling) or less than human (losing interest in life or stagnated in some addictive behavior)."[11]

Shame, and to some degree guilt, can become baggage we carry—baggage that weighs down our spiritual and emotional selves. Guilt and shame are toxic emotions that keep you from being the person God wants you to be. His desire for us is to be free from this unhealthy baggage that drags us down. Shame will keep us in bondage, but God wants to set us free from the legacy of past mistakes and painful experiences that keep us from enjoying the abundant life Jesus promised His followers (John 10:10). That promise is for all of us, no matter what.

The writer of Hebrews reminds us that when God promised to establish this new covenant with the people of Israel, He said, "No longer will they teach their neighbor, or say to one another, 'Know the Lord,' because they will all know me, from the least of them to the greatest" (Hebrews 8:11 NIV). It doesn't matter what you've done or where you've been in your life; you can know the Lord and move forward with Him.

No Longer

Don't let your past paralyze you. The tension recognized in the book of Hebrews is about which system of righteousness would be the model for the community: would it be the Levitical system that lay behind them, or the system before them, centered on Christ and His atoning sacrifice on the cross? The old system required a kind of formal, legalistic adherence to a set of 613 rules and rituals, while the new one swapped all this for forgiveness by the grace of God. The old system produced shame; the new system produces trust. The old system caused guilt; the new system creates hope.

Because of the burdens created by the old model, Christ promised to overturn that shame-inducing system, and replace it with one that emphasized peace, love, and mercy. What grabs my attention in Hebrews 8:11 are the words "no longer." The writer said that instead of merely learning about God, as under the old system, you can know Him personally.

There is a sense here of reaching a crossroads. Like those early readers, have you have reached a point where you must make up your mind to turn things around? "No longer" will we allow the tyranny of the past to cause us trauma in the present. "No longer" will we allow the lies of the enemy that held us down to keep us down. "No longer" will we allow what is behind us to prevent us from possessing what is in front of us.

No longer am I going to allow what someone said prevent me from realizing what God has said. No longer am I going to be held down, put down, and kept down by negative thoughts, unhealthy habits, trifling people, or toxic beliefs. You reach a point when you say to yourself, "No matter how bad things are, no matter how badly people treat me, I am not going to allow low-down people to bring me down." As Fannie Lou Hamer said, "I am sick and tired of being sick and tired, and we want a change."[12]

It's a Choice

You can't allow what happened to you to get the best of you. Paul expressed it this way:

> Not that I have already obtained this or have already reached the goal; but I press on to make it my own, because Christ Jesus has made me his own. Beloved, I do not consider that I have made it my own; but this one thing I do: forgetting what lies behind and straining forward to what lies ahead, I press on toward the goal for the prize of the heavenly call of God in Christ Jesus.
> **—Philippians 3:12–14** NRSV

What a powerful declaration: "I'm not going to allow what happened to me to get the best of me! I'm not going to allow what they did to me, what they said to me, what they planned and plotted against me, to cause me to give up on what God has for me." There is a sense that the key factor in recovering from brokenness is a choice. You have to choose to get better; you have to choose to be healed. You have to choose to be free.

And the reason you should make that choice is because Jesus doesn't allow what you did or what happened in your past to prevent Him from unleashing His blessings on you. I thank God that Jesus sees my mess but doesn't hold my mess against me.

God Can Handle It

I said earlier that my vacation with the kids didn't get off to a good start. That day after checking in, I was left with a new dilemma: how to get all those bags to the top of the hill to our room. It was a crazy scene.

There I was, struggling with all my bags, when the bellman came up to me and said, "Sir, please let me take that for you." I said, "No thanks," because I was trying to save a few dollars, thinking it would cost to pay this guy to carry our luggage.

The bellman said, "Sir, didn't you pay for the all-inclusive package?" I said yes. He said, "Well, included in the package is a resort fee, which means that all the amenities and benefits are free—including our baggage concierge service. We will carry your bags up to your room and bring them down when you leave; if you need to leave the resort and come back, we will hold your bags for you. There is no need for you to carry your bags to your room. It's already been paid for."

That's what I want to tell you: you don't have to carry that burden of sadness, guilt, shame, and unforgiveness. You don't have to carry that emotional baggage. It has already been paid for.

How do I know?

But He was wounded for our transgressions, He was bruised for our iniquities; the chastisement for our peace

was *upon Him, and by His stripes we are healed.*
        —*Isaiah 53:5* NKJV

God can carry it. He can handle your baggage. That's why Jesus said:

> *Come unto me, all ye that labor and are heavy laden, and I will give you rest.*
>
> *Take my yoke upon you, and learn of me; for I am meek and lowly in heart: and ye shall find rest unto your souls.*
>
> *For my yoke is easy, and my burden is light.*
>   —*Matthew 11:28–30* KJV

And there I was, carrying baggage I didn't have to carry, because the price had already been paid.

WORKBOOK

Chapter Two Questions

Question: Think back over some of the mistakes and painful experiences in your life. What emotional baggage are you still carrying? How does this affect you today? In what ways does this impact those around you?

_____

_____

_____

_____

_____

_____

_____

_____

_____

_____

Question: One of the main ways the past continues to impact us is that we believe lies about ourselves that tell us of our guilt or inadequacy. What are some of the lies you secretly believe? How have they made you into the person you are today?

_____

_____

_____

_____

_____

_____

_____

_____

_____

_____

Question: What would it take for you to be able to put down the baggage you're still carrying? How would that make you feel?

_____

_____

_____

_____

_____

_____

_____

_____

_____

_____

_____

Action: The passage in Hebrews talks about the new covenant of forgiveness by the grace of God. Jesus' death and resurrection mean we no longer have to carry around our emotional burdens. Despite what we may have believed for years, He tells us that we are precious and valued in His sight. List some ways you can hand over your baggage and begin to see yourself as He does.

Chapter Two Notes

_____

_____

_____

_____

_____

_____

_____

_____

_____

_____

_____

_____

_____

_____

_____

_____

_____

_____

_____

_____

CHAPTER THREE

Forgive Yourself

In November 2013 the movie *Frozen* was released.[13] It was everywhere, and if you were a parent with little ones, you couldn't get away from it.

The character Elsa sings a song that became a smash hit, sung by kids and adults alike—a powerful, poignant anthem entitled, "Let It Go." In my mind, I can still see my daughters, Ava and Leah, sitting in the back of the car belting out the refrain at the top of their lungs: "Let it go, let it go!" If you had a child in your house at this time, you know the words and the tune, because you heard it a thousand times.

But that song really blessed me because I interpret the lyrics as a reminder that you can't walk in the purpose and power God has for you until you "let it go." Elsa learned the hard yet necessary lesson that holding on to past hurts, mistakes, problems, and drama does nothing but hold you down. It's not until you learn to let go of the shame and fear associated with your past that you can truly live and walk into a more hopeful future.

Letting Unforgiveness Go

In the previous chapter, I talked about the baggage we carry from our pasts. And the truth is, if you want to deal with the baggage in your life, a big part of letting it go is forgiving yourself. Many people, I find, are weighed down by unforgiveness. Something happened that has broken their spirit, but the unforgiveness is what is doing them so much harm.

Engineer, scientist, mathematician, and scholar Alfred Korzybski helped popularize the maxim, "God may forgive your sins, but your nervous system won't."[14] This maxim is saying that when you've done something "wrong," your nervous system keeps track of it, causing you to feel guilty or inadequate. You tell yourself: "I'm such a loser," "I'm always doing the wrong things," "I'll never be able to lose weight," or "I'll never be able to cover my bills." If you thought forgiving others is difficult, forgiving yourself is even harder.

Many of us live weighed down by the failings and failures in our pasts: rehearsing what we did, reliving and rehashing the event over and over again. And that's what keeps the unforgiveness fresh in your life and in your mind.

But God says, "I've come to set you free from the pain, so you don't have to keep beating yourself up about it." In Psalm 103:12 (NRSV), we read that "as far as the east is from the west, so far [God] removes our transgressions from us." You don't have to punish yourself any longer, because when Jesus shed His blood, He paid the price for your sins once and for all. All you have to do is let it go.

King with a Secret

Blessed is the one whose transgressions are forgiven, whose sins are covered. Blessed is the one whose sin the LORD does not count against them and in whose spirit is no deceit.

When I kept silent, my bones wasted away through my groaning all day long. For day and night your hand was heavy on me; my strength was sapped as in the heat of summer.

Then I acknowledged my sin to you and did not cover up my iniquity. I said, "I will confess my transgressions to the LORD." And you forgave the guilt of my sin.

Therefore let all the faithful pray to you while you may be found; surely the rising of the mighty waters will not reach them. You are my hiding place; you will protect me from trouble and surround me with songs of deliverance.

Rejoice in the LORD and be glad, you righteous; sing, all you who are upright in heart!
                                          —Psalm 32:1–7, 11 NIV

If anyone was acquainted with the need to forgive oneself, it was king David from the Old Testament. Psalm 32 (quoted above) was written by David, a mostly righteous and God-fearing king, following a series of misdeeds and immoral acts he had committed. In the most infamous incident, David saw Bathsheba bathing on a rooftop and began an affair with her (2 Samuel 11). When she became pregnant, David tried to cover up his adulterous act by bringing her husband home from battle, hoping that he would sleep with his wife and believe that the child was his.

But Uriah refused to indulge in pleasure while his comrades remained on the battlefield, so David decided to have him killed in battle. He ordered the commander to place Uriah on the front line and then withdraw support from him. The plan worked, and Uriah died.

King David, the man after God's own heart (Acts 13:22), had a man killed to cover up his own sinful act and tried to go on living as if nothing had happened. But what's done in the dark will always come to light. David had hidden his dastardly deed from everyone else, but he couldn't hide from God or His prophet Nathan.

For perhaps the first time in his life, the shepherd boy turned king was confronted with his own pride and the realization that he was forfeiting the glory and presence of God because of what he had done. He humbled himself and poured out this prayer, found in Psalm 51:12 (KJV): "Restore unto me the joy of thy salvation; and uphold me with thy free spirit."

When you read the story of David's confrontation with the prophet Nathan in 2 Samuel 12, you discover the truth that what God has ahead of us far outweighs what lies behind us—but, to experience it and receive it, like David we have to let go of the past.

There are many "Davids," or those of us who have done things we regret. Here's the thing: the first person many of us need to forgive is ourselves. Everyone talks about living their best life, but are you really doing that if

you haven't forgiven yourself for the mistake you made
ten years ago?

Healing Through Forgiveness

The good news of the text is that despite David's sinful
act, God still forgave him. Only God can provide freedom
in a world that will hold you hostage to mistakes made
twenty years ago—wrong choices made out of broken situations, regretful words said out of unvoiced pain. For if
Christ makes you free, you are free indeed (John 8:36).
The lesson is to not let what you did keep you from what
God wants you to do. Don't let what happened hinder
what God wants to happen. You can be free if you just let
it go. Forgive yourself.

I too have struggled to forgive myself. When I had a
falling out with someone close to me and they passed
away, I wished that I would have communicated with
them earlier. However, not having the closure I believed I
needed created an anxiety within me that was difficult to
release.

Like me, many people struggle with guilt; it can destroy your life. The journey back toward health,
wholeness, and healing comes when you reach a point
where you can forgive yourself and let go of the things
you cannot change. That can only happen when you realize God has forgiven you: "Blessed is the one whose
transgressions are forgiven, whose sins are covered.
Blessed is the one whose sin the LORD does not count
against them" (Psalm 32:1–2 NIV). The good news of the

text begins with the recognition that even when we have transgressed God's will and God's way, He forgives us.

In Isaiah 43:25 (NRSV), God says, "I, I am He who blots out your transgressions for my own sake, and I will not remember your sins."

Elsewhere we read, "He does not retain his anger forever, because he delights in showing clemency. He will again have compassion upon us; he will tread our iniquities under foot. You will cast all our sins into the depths of the sea" (Micah 7:18b–19 NRSV). And, "if we confess our sins, he who is faithful and just will forgive us our sins and cleanse us from all unrighteousness" (1 John 1:9 NRSV).

The Bible is clear: you are forgiven.

Letting Go of the Guilt

Knowing that you are forgiven by God helps you to forgive yourself. But that's not always easy, because we are used to carrying our heavy psychological burden. That's why forgiving yourself involves the practical step of letting go of the negative emotions you've been holding on to. In fact, psychologists often define forgiveness as a "deliberate decision to release feelings of resentment and vengeance."[15] We saw an example of that in Psalm 32. To experience the freedom God had for him, David had to take some steps to release all the pain, guilt, and shame that had built up from his past.

Look at verses 3 and 4: "When I kept silent, my bones wasted away through my groaning all day long. For day and night your hand was heavy upon me; my strength was sapped as in the heat of summer" (NRSV). David was talking about the effort of trying to hide what he had done and hold everything in. He was overcome with guilt. His body was feeling the weight of his actions, and he discovered that trying to bury it was slowly destroying him. To be set free from the chains of his guilt and shame, he had to release his past to God. Even though what he had done was heinous and horrible, he realized he had to let it go. He could have spent a lot of time blaming others or making excuses for why he did what he did, but he reached a point where he realized he had to stop hiding and turn it all over to God.

How did he do that? Psalm 51 gives us some clues. David asked for mercy. He prayed for his guilt to be washed away and asked God to create a pure heart within him. He believed in God's forgiveness and began to praise Him.

God had forgiven David, but he now had to forgive himself. God freed David from eternal punishment, but he now had to free himself from earthly punishment—the torment of guilt. It was keeping him in bondage to his past and preventing him from walking in his destiny.

Sometimes we don't forgive ourselves because we are holding on to an underlying emotion or belief. We feel, at some level, that we don't deserve forgiveness or that we don't have the right to let go of the guilt. Sometimes we feel we are unlovable. And sometimes that underlying belief is, "Well, maybe I did something to deserve this." These are all lies the enemy uses to keep us down.

You have to identify the belief or the emotion that is preventing you from forgiving yourself, and decide to turn the page.

I've noticed a trend with my kids. Before they eat or drink anything in my house, they always look at the expiration dates. It really started to irk me, but they said, "Dad, you have a tendency to hold on to food after it has expired, and we don't want to get sick because you refuse to throw things out." Have you ever held on to something longer than you should have? Pants? A shirt? What about milk? It's spoiled, it's gone bad, and it smells.

Some of you are holding on to pain, hurt, and guilt from your past and it's time to let it go. Some of you are where David was: sad, depressed, and struggling to move forward in life. God says, "Stop holding on to things that are well past their expiration date! Throw it out, and let it go. Let go of the mistakes; let go of the grudges; let go of the guilt; let go of the shame."

Listen, child of God, cut yourself some slack! Give yourself permission to make mistakes. We are all fallible. The Bible says all of us have sinned and fall short of the glory of God (Romans 3:23). Note that this verse says "fall short," in the present tense. We all make mistakes in the present, but those mistakes can make us wiser. They are a part of being human. Acceptance can lead to the emotional healing you are looking for, so bring your mistakes to God and leave them in His hands.

No Condemnation

It's time for you to free yourself and forgive yourself for what's happened in your past. So many people haven't forgiven themselves for something they did, or even for something that was done to them. They are held hostage by a choice they made, and it keeps them from moving forward.

It is the devil, and not God, who seeks to bring con demnation into your life. It is he, not God, who seeks to sow seeds of guilt, shame, embarrassment, and disgrace. He is the one who wants you to think that what you have done is so bad that you are beyond redemption and beyond restoration.

But the apostle Paul said in Romans 8:1, "There is therefore now no condemnation for those who are in Christ Jesus" (NRSV). Whatever you have done, whatever you said, whatever happened, God loves you so much that He doesn't hold grudges. He doesn't hold what you did against you. You are forgiven.

To be forgiven by God is no doubt life's greatest blessing. Without it, there can be no real joy, no real peace, no real contentment, and no hope. Forgiveness is what puts hope in the heart, peace in the mind, and a song in the soul, and it alone brings us closer to God. Forgiveness opens the door of deliverance and restoration. It reveals the majesty of God's mercy, the sufficiency of God's grace, and the depth of God's marvelous love. God's forgiveness reaches out to us all.

No matter who we are, no matter where we live, no matter what we may have done, no matter how vile, corrupt, immoral, rebellious, or hateful, God says, "I'll give you another chance." Other people may not, but God will. Others may punish us, but God pardons us.

So don't let what you did separate you from the presence, the power, and the peace of God. God has given you another chance, and that's something to rejoice about.

He's never stopped caring for you, watching out for you, or loving you. No matter what you have done, nothing can keep you from the love of God.

Paul also said, in Romans 8:38–39 (NRSV), "For I am convinced that neither death, nor life, nor angels, nor rulers, nor things present, nor things to come, nor powers, nor height, nor depth, nor anything else in all creation, will be able to separate us from the love of God in Christ Jesus our Lord."

Like a lamp in a window on a dark night, God's light of forgiveness is always on, welcoming you home if you just acknowledge what you did, repent, and turn to Him.

Blessed Assurance

Once David released the guilt of his past, he was reassured of God's plan of redemption.

David trusted God. He believed God's promise. He knew he was not perfect, but that God is. He knew he made mistakes, but he also knew that his God could blot out his transgressions. And because of that, he had blessed assurance. Psalm 32:5 says that David brought his transgressions to God and God forgave the guilt of his sin. God not only forgave the sinful act and cleared the slate, but He also got rid of the guilt, the regret, and all the other emotions that come with sin. God is thorough; He doesn't cut corners. When He forgives, He does it all the way. It gave David a new walk and a new talk; his shame was turned into a smile, his lament into new life.

And God can do the same thing for you and for me. God specializes in renewing our lives and giving us a new sense of purpose. He promises to guide us, keep us, and lead us, because He loves us, despite what we've done. And if God loves me, I'm going to love myself. If God cares for me, I'm going to care for myself. If God forgives me, I'm going to forgive myself. God's loving eye is not one of disdain or criticism. He doesn't believe in exclusion or labels, but in inclusion, redemption, and healing. God doesn't allow what's behind you to keep you from grasping what's ahead of you.

Forgive yourself. It's the toughest thing you will ever do. God's forgiveness means open arms, second chances, slates wiped clean, and regeneration. Life can begin again, beauty can flourish, communities can grow, relationships can be healed. Here's the promise of Jesus in Matthew 11:28: "Come unto me, all ye that labor and are heavy laden, and I will give you rest" (KJV). God calls you to let it go so that He can guide you. Let it go so that you can walk fully in His promises. Let it go so that you can live in peace. Let it go, because the price has already been paid for you to fully receive forgiveness, newness, and love.

Chapter Three Questions

Question: We've all made mistakes and done things in the past we're ashamed of. Why do you think it's hard to put them behind us and let go? What would change in your life if you could learn to put down this burden?

_____

_____

_____

_____

_____

_____

_____

_____

_____

Question: The Scriptures make it clear that God is ready to forgive us, but sometimes we're not so ready to repent. What happens when we try to conceal our sin, like David?

_____

_____

_____

_____

_____

_____

_____

_____

_____

_____

Question: What kind of things do you find it hard to forgive yourself for? Ask God to show you the secret beliefs that keep you from experiencing freedom. What lies has the enemy been telling you?

_____

_____

_____

_____

_____

_____

_____

_____

_____

_____

Action: Experiencing God's forgiveness and letting go of the past are key steps to healing negative emotions and painful memories. How can you take these steps in your life?

Chapter Three Notes

_____

_____

_____

_____

_____

_____

_____

_____

_____

_____

_____

_____

_____

_____

_____

_____

_____

_____

_____

_____

_____

CHAPTER FOUR

I'm Under the Influence

Stuart Briscoe told the story of a young man who did not like taking direction from others.[16] On his eighteenth birthday, this young man asked his dad for the car keys so that he could go out and celebrate with his friends. His father replied, "It's a school night; we want you home by 10:30 p.m." The young man said, "I'm eighteen years old now. Nobody can tell me what to do." To which the father said, "Okay, it is getting hard to tell you what to do. But I'm keeping the keys, and you can walk to be with your friends."

The next day, the young man went to football practice at school, but he got there late. When the coach saw him coming out on the field late, he told him to do thirty pushups. And he said, "Coach, I'm eighteen years old now. Nobody can tell me what to do." And the coach said, "Okay, if that's the way you want it, you're off the team."

The young man now had extra time on his hands, so he got a job after school. But one day, the boss told him to sweep up a mess. He didn't believe that was part of his job description, so he said, "I'm eighteen years old now. Nobody can tell me what to do." And the boss said, "That's your choice, but if that's your attitude, you're fired."

Then, one of his teachers asked him to turn in his research paper, and you know what he said? "I'm eighteen years old now. Nobody can tell me what to do." The teacher said, "That's your choice, but you get an F for the course."

After he dropped out of school, he joined the army in hopes of having freedom from all the people who tried to tell him what to do at home. On the third day of boot camp, the drill sergeant ran them to exhaustion and then told them to do another fifty pushups. The young man said, "Listen, sergeant, I'm eighteen years old now. Nobody can tell me what to do." I really can't tell you what the drill sergeant said, but you can use your imagination.

The young man had to discover that as much as he wanted to be in control of his life, situations come along where you have to give up control and yield to a higher power. In a real sense, that's the lesson from Paul's letter to the Ephesians:

> *Take no part in the unfruitful works of darkness, but instead expose them. For it is shameful even to mention what such people do secretly; but everything exposed by the light becomes visible, for everything that becomes visible is light. Therefore, it says,*

> *"Sleeper, awake! Rise from the dead, and Christ will shine on you."*

*Be very careful, then, how you live, not as unwise people
but as wise, making the most of the time, because the days
are evil. So do not be foolish, but understand what the will
of the Lord is. Do not get drunk with wine, for that is debauchery; but be filled with the Spirit....*

--Ephesians 5:11–18 NRSV

Once we get saved and begin to live for Jesus Christ,
we relinquish control. We've been bought with a price, so
that the Holy Spirit within us now takes control and command over us. Greater victory comes for Christians when
we learn to walk in the authority and by the power given
to us in Jesus Christ. The very day that you and I re-
sponded to the gospel and accepted Jesus Christ as our
personal Lord and Savior, we were adopted into the family of God; and as such, we became heirs of the promise,
purpose, and power made available to us in Jesus Christ.
That life-giving, life-sustaining, life-changing power is
the power of the Holy Spirit.

The Holy Spirit is a guide. The Bible says the Holy
Spirit guides us into all truth and intercedes for us (John
16:13; Romans 8:26). That's why Paul calls us to be filled
with the influence of the Spirit, to yield our lives to His
guidance and comfort. Yet most of us can't be filled with
the Spirit, because we don't understand why we need
Him.

Influence of the Comforter

The book of Ephesians lays out the rights and privi-
leges of those who have been adopted into the family of
God. And a part of the promise requires us, as God's

children, to lay down the right to be carnally controlled, in exchange for being Spirit-controlled. It says in verse 18, "Do not get drunk with wine, for that is debauchery; but be filled with the Spirit" (NRSV). The writer, Paul, wanted readers to understand that God had a purpose for them that could be accomplished if they would rely on a strength, ability, and power that was not their own. Paul said it is essential to be controlled by the spiritual presence within you.

According to Jesus, the Christian life is absolutely impossible apart from the power of the Holy Spirit. Jesus said in John 15:5 that "apart from me you can do nothing" (NRSV). He was saying we need to be under the influence of a power that will transform the world around us. To be under the influence of the Spirit is to be controlled by the Spirit, to be guided in the Spirit, and to be led by the Spirit.

Every child of God should be able to say unapologetically that they are under the influence of the Spirit, are led by the Spirit, and are driven by the Spirit. Unfortunately, talk about the Holy Spirit in the church, especially in certain parts of the Christian family, has been marred with a great deal of controversy and confusion. The way the Holy Spirit is presented and experienced in some quarters has caused many people to become scared of the Spirit.

The indwelling of the Holy Spirit is about the presence and power of God working on the inside to give us clarity, confidence, and counsel on the outside. Paul says to be filled with a different energy, a unique force, and an exclusive power. You are called to embody a different presence than that of others. Your life is influenced by a different power.

There is nothing that can so affect the lifestyle, the habits, the character, the testimony, the desires, and the attitudes of a genuine Christian more than the outpouring, the infilling, and the overflowing of the Holy Spirit. To the growing Christian, being filled with the Holy Spirit is much more than a novelty; it is a necessity. It is more than a part of God's elective courses; it is the core curriculum. It is not something for your convenience. It is a requirement.

If you are going to be victorious over your circumstances instead of becoming a victim to them, you must yield to the Spirit's reality and presence in your life. Without the fullness of the Spirit, you will remain weak in your faith, stunted in your spiritual growth, and frustrated in your walk. For the saints, there are many times when dreary days, long hours, feeble knees, and difficult trials can cause us to feel alone, but thanks be to God that He has not left us. He has not abandoned us to face raging storms, climb rough mountains, or endure difficult days by ourselves.

In fact, in John 16:7, Jesus said that He must leave in order that the Comforter might come. He comes to be your guide, your counselor, your defense, your strength, your support, your companion, and your shield. Jesus also said to His disciples, "But the Comforter, which is the Holy Ghost, whom the Father will send in my name, he shall teach you all things, and bring all things to your remembrance, whatsoever I have said unto you." (John 14:26 KJV).

When no one else is there, God's Spirit is there. When everyone else walks away from you, God's Spirit is by your side, strengthening you when you are weak, assuring you when you are uncertain, healing you when you are hurt, and blessing you when you are burdened.

Being filled does not mean that you get more of the Spirit, but that the Spirit gets more of you. The Holy Spirit does not need you, but you desperately, absolutely, and unequivocally need Him.

Bringers of Light

The text, Ephesians 5:11–18, suggests that when you are truly under the influence of the Spirit, you bring light to dark places. It would be easy to think that Paul wrote this letter from the comfort of a temple, but he didn't; he wrote it while chained in prison. Talk about a dark place! From that place of darkness Paul proclaimed:

> *Take no part in the unfruitful works of darkness, but instead expose them. For it is shameful even to mention what such people do secretly; but everything exposed by the light becomes visible, for everything that becomes visible is light.*
> **—Ephesians 5:11–14a** NRSV

The power of the Holy Spirit prevented the darkness of prison from limiting the light that God placed within Paul. Rather than allowing the difficulty and darkness of his situation to overwhelm him, the power of the Holy Spirit strengthened him. The real job of the Holy Spirit in your life is to be an internal generator providing light to dark spaces.

An old popular saying is that "it is far better to light a candle than to curse the darkness."[17] We are living in dark times where truth is overlooked, poverty is ignored, bigotry is emboldened, and hate and indecency are widespread. Yet rather than being overcome by the dark, if we let our lights shine bright, we can overcome the darkness. God didn't save us, empower us, and fill us with His Spirit to be a light only in our homes and churches, and in the safe confines of spaces that are already well lit. Instead, God saved us to be His ambassadors of light in places where there is no light.

One night when I arrived home, I noticed one of the lights in front of my house wasn't working. The next evening, remembering to replace it, I went out to change the bulb. To my astonishment, the light wasn't broken; rather, it was covered in bugs! They were so attracted to the light that they completely covered it. The light was there all along, but what was around it had dimmed and diminished its brightness. I didn't need to replace anything. I needed to beat off the bugs blocking the light that was already shining. That's what many of us need to do in our lives. We need to beat off the bugs and the things around us that are blocking the light that we already have.

That's what the Holy Spirit does. He helps to ward off the things trying to block our light. When you're under the influence of the Holy Spirit, you bring light to dark places.

Walking Wisely

Ephesians 5 also says that when you're under the influence of the Spirit, you don't waste your time on things, activities, and associations that don't matter. You're on assignment! Paul told the Ephesians not to waste their time walking around the unwise. "See then that you walk circumspectly, not as fools but as wise, redeeming the time, because the days are evil" (Ephesians 5:15–16 NKJV).

You cannot leave the Christian life to chance. You must make wise decisions and seek to do the will of God. This point about not wasting time is really connected with purpose. Paul seems to have been saying, "Don't walk in your sleep! Wake up! Open your eyes! Make the most of the day!"

It is sad to see many professed Christians drift through life like sleepwalkers; they never really make the most of opportunities to live for Christ and serve Him. Paul warned them to walk wisely. *Wise walking* is walking with a purpose and a destination. It's being guided by the Spirit and not by your own impulses.

Two ways to get to a destination include 1) traveling alone and figuring it out yourself or 2) having someone with knowledge guide you. Jesus said that "when the Spirit of truth comes, he will guide you into all the truth" (John 16:13 NRSV). Too many of us waste time in life because, instead of following the way of wisdom and a path of purpose, we forge our path alone, following the way of the flesh. We choose someone based upon appearance rather than anointing, or we favor cash rather than character. The Holy Spirit in your life helps you to make wise choices.

In yielding to the Holy Spirit, He gives you discernment and keeps you from living without standards, wasting your time on trivial things, and compromising your dreams for people, places, and things that are beneath your potential.

Paul didn't want to be found wasting his time on anything that distracted him or took him away from the path and assignment God had him on. He wanted to make sure that his people and his church were ready for the Lord's arrival. Paul knew that if they were going to prepare for what was coming, they could not allow themselves to get distracted by what had already been. To be light shiners, they couldn't be time wasters.

When you are under your own influence rather than the Spirit's, you do things your way instead of God's way, and that's what gets many of us in trouble. Because they are not Spirit-led, many people find themselves wasting time; their time, energy, and resources are spent on the wrong people, the wrong investments, and the wrong things.

Filled with the Spirit

Paul instructed the Ephesians not to drink in excess— not to be overindulgent in that which brings temporary satisfaction, but rather to be filled with the Spirit. It is the Spirit who helps to temper your desires so that your wants do not become overdependent on the external realities of life. Many of us have overindulged in a whole host of behaviors. For example, some people are drunk with power, drunk with credit cards, or drunk with sex, while others are drunk with laziness.

When you have the Spirit, you're not controlled by the circumstances or the pleasures of the world. The Holy Spirit helps you to say no when you want to say yes, and to walk away from something you would normally walk into. The Bible says that a fruit of the Spirit is *self-control*, which is the ability to exercise self-command and restrain oneself.[18]

But the Holy Spirit doesn't only keep us from being consumed by pleasure. He also helps us withstand difficulty, trials, and suffering. Remember, when Paul wrote this, he was in prison and many believers were facing the threat of persecution and death. Yet Paul spoke as one with confident strength, because what he had on the inside was greater than what was happening on the outside.

When you have God with you, nothing you face can overtake you. That's why, in his closing verse, he told them to sing and to make melody with all their hearts. Paul was not trying to get them to sing for the sake of singing, but rather to cultivate an inner joy to express gratitude and trust in God. You can do the same thing. You can have joy in difficulty knowing you have within you a divine partner, a heavenly helper, to assist you in times of trouble.

And the good news is that the Holy Spirit isn't something you have to work for, once you get saved. It's not something you have qualify for. All of us, when we accept Christ and are baptized, freely receive the Holy Spirit. I often struggled with that as a young Christian. I heard people telling me I needed a power, but I didn't have the power because I didn't at the time have a manifestation of the Spirit, whether it was speaking in tongues or manifesting some other outward sign. But as I grew in Christ, I realized that the Holy Spirit wasn't something I had to get. I was already baptized and filled with the Spirit from the moment I had given my life to Jesus.

When you become a believer, God places the Holy Spirit within you, and He will teach you to listen and respond to the Spirit's counsel. If you are saved, don't let anyone convince you that you don't have the Holy Spirit residing inside you.

I'm a manuscript preacher, and I recall years ago, when my sermon notes were written by hand, looking frantically around my apartment for my notes one morning before I had to preach. I looked everywhere. I looked under my bed; I looked in my desk drawer; I even went outside to look in my car.

After a long, futile search, I had to get to the church where I was speaking. I grabbed my keys and went there exhausted, frustrated, and incredibly nervous because I didn't have the sermon notes I so desperately needed. When I got up to speak, I said a quick prayer: "Lord, I don't know what's going to happen right now, but I need You to give me something to say to these people." As I stood at the mic, I opened my Bible to the passage I wanted to preach from, and there in the pages of my Bible were my notes. I had been exhausting myself trying to find something I already had.

Don't frustrate yourself listening to other people's theologies about the Holy Spirit. There's nothing more frustrating than searching for something you already have. As a believer, you already have the help you need. You already have the strength you need. You already have the power you need. The Holy Spirit is the rain that refreshes, the fire that warms, the seal that secures, and the river that satisfies. He gives you everything you need if you ask and remain open to Him, so you can confidently say, "I'm under the influence of the Holy Spirit."

WORKBOOK

Chapter Four Questions

Question: We are all "under the influence" of whatever drives us and controls us. What have been some of the main influences in your life?

_____

_____

_____

_____

_____

_____

_____

_____

_____

_____

_____

Question: Being filled with the Spirit involves allowing Him to be in charge, to lead and direct us. Do you find that idea liberating or constricting? Does it scare you or excite you? Explain why.

_____

_____

_____

_____

_____

_____

_____

_____

_____

_____

Question: In what ways does your light shine out to others? What are some of the dark corners you can bring light to?

_____

_____

_____

_____

_____

_____

_____

_____

_____

_____

_____

_____

Action: What are some practical ways you can give control of your daily decisions regarding lifestyle, relationships, and career over to the Holy Spirit?

Chapter Four Notes

CHAPTER FIVE

I'm Getting My Energy Back

At the 2014 St. Anthony's Marathon in Italy, a Kenyan runner by the name of Eliud Magut, one of the favorites to win the marathon, literally pushed himself to the limit and gave out. In the video that went viral across the internet, Magut fell and got up three times, only to collapse just yards before the finish line.[19] This happens when the body is pushed to limits it is not intended to go. When people keep running and running and running, the body becomes depleted of the energy, strength, and fuel it needs to press on. And in the end, it breaks down—it literally collapses. Despite their desire to press on, the person is unable to do anything else.

The body is like a machine, and any machinery that runs and runs without any rest, without any replenishment, will exceed its capacity to function and will break down. Whether it's the engine in your car that never gets an oil change, or the air conditioner in your house that never has its filter changed, when machines like your body work too hard, they reach a point where they get clogged. When that happens, the machine will work harder and harder until it eventually runs out of steam and stops working.

You may know what that's like in your own life: you've been doing so much that the weight of your responsibilities and the busyness of your schedule have caused you to reach a point where you feel like it's just too much, and you can't take it anymore. Between work, family, church, and other commitments, you feel like you're burning the candle of your life at both ends, and quite frankly, you're exhausted, tired, and low on energy.

And in the mix, your spiritual life is getting compromised. You don't pray like you should; you don't worship with the kind of intimacy that you need. You only read the Bible verses the preacher cites on Sunday.

What's the remedy? A shift in priorities. You've got to be so laser-focused on your purpose, your assignment, your destiny, and your future, that you are more interested in pleasing God than pleasing people.

Is Your Strength Sapped?

Centuries before Christ, God spoke through the prophet Jeremiah. He promised, "I will satisfy the weary, and all who are faint I will replenish" (Jeremiah 31:25 NRSV). Or, as another version puts it, "I'll refresh tired bodies; I'll restore tired souls" (MSG). He was addressing people whose strength had been completely sapped out of them by the journey of life. They were at the point of giving up because they had no more energy.

This passage is interesting because it suggests that God doesn't regard running on empty as a spiritual value or a personal achievement. Some people think that there's something holy about always appearing to be run down. No, God says, if your body is tired, do something about it. If your soul is not rested, restore it. I think that's because God doesn't just want us to survive where we are; He wants us to thrive where we are. He wants us to get our energy back.

The Answer to Burnout and Stress

Who is setting the pace in your life right now? Is it society, your boss, your spouse, your circle of friends? Is it your emotions and feelings? Are you following your agenda or God's? Did you buy a bigger house not because your family grew or you really needed one, but because you saw your friend's new house, and your stress is related to wanting to have what they have?

Jesus said, "Come to me, all you who are weary and burdened, and I will give you rest. Take my yoke upon you and learn from me, for I am gentle and humble in heart, and you will find rest for your souls. For my yoke is easy and my burden is light" (Matthew 11:28–30 NIV). If Jesus is your pacesetter, if you take His yoke upon you, you won't be burdened trying to keep up with the Joneses.

The problem with trying to keep up with the Joneses is that it's always a moving target. The Joneses are trying to keep up with the Jacksons, and the Jacksons are trying to keep up with the Jeffersons. Now people are trying to keep up with the Kardashians.

Burnout happens when you try to take on more things and tasks than you are able to handle; you keep adding more and more responsibilities to your "to do" list, and it just becomes too much. Perhaps you have to do everything yourself.

Have you ever been riding in the car with someone and it was clear that you were lost, but you wouldn't pull over and ask for directions because you didn't want to admit you didn't know?

Once I was at the gym doing some bench presses, and there were guys next to me lifting. I thought, "Hey, these guys are younger than me, and I'm not going to let them show me up." So I decided to put whatever weight on my bar that I saw on theirs. And man, they kept adding more and more weight, but my ego wouldn't let me stop. I ended up embarrassing myself, with the bar crashing down on my chest, because I wasn't willing to admit when I had reached my limit.

The underlying myth that fuels burnout is the idea that you self-determine your future. And while this may make for good poetry and literature and music, it's bad theology because it causes us to think that if the going gets tough, we just have to bear down and get tougher. Oftentimes when we are overwhelmed, when we are weighed down, we turn inward and tell ourselves we can handle it. We tell ourselves we just need to work harder, put in a few extra hours, and dig deeper. But this is an illusion.

Jesus said that when you are physically, mentally, and spiritually worn out, you don't have to handle it yourself—you can come to Him. He tells us that the solution for an overloaded soul is not a plan, not a process, but a person. And that person is Him. Jesus says, "Come to me. Rather than trying to do it all yourself, come to Me. Give it to Me. Recognize your limitations."

It's okay to ask for help. It's okay to say no to people every now and then. It's okay to say, "I'd love to, but I can't right now." It's okay to admit to yourself and others that you don't have the capacity to do it all yourself. I know you're smart. I know you're educated. I know you have a fancy job with a big title, but it's okay to admit that you've reached your limit.

Moses had to understand that, too. After God brought the Israelites out of slavery in Egypt to lead them to the Promised Land, they spent years wandering through the desert. Moses was responsible for two million people (Numbers 11 and Exodus 18), and he got overwhelmed and stressed out. He said, "I am not able to carry all this people alone, for they are too heavy for me" (Numbers 11:14 NRSV).

What had happened? He got overwhelmed because he had bought into the myth of invincibility. In Exodus 18, we read how he alone tried to resolve every problem the people brought to him. Then one day, his father-in-law Jethro said to him, "What you are doing is not good. You will surely wear yourself out, both you and these people with you. For the task is too heavy for you; you cannot do it alone" (Exodus 18:17–18 NRSV). Essentially, Jethro told him he needed to get some help.

Don't buy into the false premise that it can't happen without you, whatever your "it" is. Don't think that the company will not survive unless you're there, that the church cannot go on unless you are on your post, and that the organization will collapse unless you are the president.

Maybe you're at your wits' end because you've been so busy making a living that you haven't made a life. You can't do it all. That's why Jesus uses this metaphor of a yoke when he says, "Take my yoke upon you ... for my yoke is easy and my burden is light." A *yoke* is a wooden beam that attaches two farm animals together.[20] The purpose is to make the load easier. Instead of one ox or horse pulling the load, you use the yoke to have two animals carry more because they're working together.

That's what Jesus was saying: "I want you to take My yoke upon you because with Me you can do more than you can do by yourself." God never meant for you to bear the burdens of life on your own.

Psalm 55:22 tells us, "Cast your burden on the LORD, and he will sustain you; he will never permit the righteous to be moved" (NRSV). Jesus said, "Come to Me, join up with Me, and I'll help you." Yoking your life with Christ is so important because when you are yoked together with someone, you have to move in the same direction and at the same pace that they move.

Perhaps you get burned out or stressed out because you're trying to manage it all alone. But when you are going in the same direction and are living your life at the same pace as Christ, you will stress less because you know He's got your back. When you let Jesus set the pace of your life, your stress level goes down and your satisfaction level goes up.

Where Do You Need to Say No?

Restoration is at the heart of God's will for your life and mine. And for it to happen, in order for you to get your energy back, you must first determine what is draining you. Time is energy, and a lot of people are clueless about where they devote most of their time and whether the time they are spending is helping or hurting them.

In his book *Leading on Empty: Refilling Your Tank and Renewing Your Passion*, Wayne Cordeiro wrote about a revision of Psalm 23 that illustrates perfectly how overwhelmed people are today. It goes:[21]

> The clock is my dictator, I shall not rest. It makes me lie down only when exhausted. It leads me into deep depression, it hounds my soul. It leads me in circles of frenzy for activities' sake. Even though I run frantically from task to task, I will never get it all done, for my "ideal" is with me. Deadlines and my need for approval, they drive me. They demand performance from me, beyond the limits of my schedule. They anoint my head with migraines, my in-basket overflows. Surely fatigue and time pressure shall follow me all the days of my life. And I will dwell in the bonds of frustration forever.

God doesn't want you to live like that! Do an energy audit so that you can know for yourself what and whom you're investing your time in, and where you're putting your energy. You can't get a sense of what to change until you can see what you're doing. You will probably discover that in many instances, you're spending most of your time and energy on others and only a little energy on yourself and on God.

The reason you need to do an energy audit is to help you determine your return on investment. Are the activities you're devoting your time to, and the relationships you're spending your time in, generating a good return on your investment, or are they just sucking all the energy out of you? All the energy you spend has to be replenished. Just like gas in a car, once the tank is empty, you have to refill it.

And to keep you from draining your energy into relationships, places, and things that aren't productive, you need to know where you're spending most of your time. Do you spend an inordinate amount of time watching TV? What about on social media? How about being engaged in conversations and arguments that really aren't going anywhere? Your energy audit will help you get a clear sense of why you may not be as spiritually productive, financially prosperous, and physically healthy as you want to be.

You can't pray and grow in the Word if you're devoting substantial hours a day to watching reality TV and scrolling through your Instagram feed. You can't make more sales in your business or find more clients if you're wasting time in relationships and friendships that don't add to your life and aren't where the Holy Spirit is directing you. In the same way, you can't exercise four times a week if you're so busy taking care of other people's problems that you are neglecting yourself.

Tom Rath, author of *Are You Fully Charged?*, said that he has asked more than ten thousand people, "Did you have a great deal of physical energy yesterday?" and just 11 percent said they did.[22] That means 89 percent of us are operating without much to spare. The fact is, you don't have time to waste doing the wrong things. If you want to get your energy back, you're going to have to be more strategic about where you spend your time.

In my own life, I had to discover that there were a lot of energy sappers I had to get rid of so that I could be more effective. When I was a student at Morehouse, I was constantly reminded of my need to be a better steward of the time and talent God had given me by hearing the words of "God's Minute," an anonymous poem regularly cited by Dr. Benjamin E. Mays, president of Morehouse College from 1940 to 1967. The poem says: "I have only a minute. Only sixty seconds in it, forced upon me—can't refuse it. Didn't seek it, didn't choose it, but it's up to me to use it. I must suffer if I lose it, give account if I abuse it. Just a tiny little minute—but eternity is in it."[23]

Knowing what's draining your energy is key because it's going to help you to focus your energy. There is tremendous power in focus; you can't be effective if you're all over the place. What causes many people to be all over the place is a sense that everything is urgent. You drop it all and run because you believe every time someone calls you, it's an emergency.

You believe everything that your momma wants you to do for her, that your friends want you to do for them, that the ministry wants you to make time for, and that your colleagues on the job want you to do are all life and death matters only you can attend to. There is this seemingly unending list of things you have to do for other people, because you have made their emergencies your emergencies.

And when you live your life that way, you find out quickly that you'll stay spiritually and physically depleted. What you have to do is develop a clear sense of focus so that you'll know what to say yes to and what to say no to.

In his book *It: How Churches and Leaders Can Get It and Keep It*, Craig Groeschel writes about the way churches get away from their mission because they confuse every good idea with a God idea. He says that every church, every organization, every leader, and every person has an assignment from God that is just for them. But a lot of people miss their destiny because they take on every good idea presented to them instead of the God idea that God has spoken to them.[24]

When you find out what your priorities are, and when you discover what your purpose is, you will experience the huge power contained in a small word. It's the word *no*. Come on. Try saying it. It will free you.

I'm not saying you shouldn't be helpful to people, and I'm not saying you should be mean, but you've got to understand what you can do and what you can't do, and you can't do everything. You must recognize your limitations.

Some of us are stressed out because we treat life like a buffet restaurant—we try to eat or do it all. You can't do it all. A picture frame has a border, and a plate has a rim, because you are not supposed to hold everything. You don't have to say yes to everyone.

Doing You

Throughout the course of my ministry, I've had to recognize my own limitations. I have colleagues in ministry whose ministry model calls for multiple church locations and many different services at each location. It is really quite impressive. They are incredibly successful. And periodically, I encounter people who suggest that I should do the same thing. However, I know my limitations. Many people get burned out emotionally and spiritually because they are insecure within themselves. They need an external source of validation. They have certain cars because they need their social circle to validate them. They constantly date and are willing to date anyone because their insecurity prevents them from being discerning and waiting for the person who is right for them.

These are people who do everything for clout. They present a false image of themselves on social media for likes and followers, but it's not real. Clout chasing will get you in trouble. Clout chasing will stress you out. And you'll never be fulfilled if you need external sources of validation. In order to be focused on God's priorities for your life, you can't be so needy. One of the reasons people spend so much time trying to be everything for everyone is because they really lack self-esteem, and their low sense of self causes them to think that if they say yes to everyone, people will like them. The emptiness they have within causes them to seek the approval, affirmation, and validation of others, and so they are constantly available to others—because they are trying to fill this hole in their soul.

Sometimes your energy is drained because you spend all your time trying to please people. And the reason you don't tell people no when you don't want to do what they are asking you to do is because you attach your self-esteem and your self-worth to whether people need you or like you, and that's never a good thing.

The reason your schedule is all over the place—you're involved in more activities than you can handle, and you don't devote as much time as you need in prayer, studying the Word, eating right, exercising, and being with your family—is that you are looking for external sources of validation when your sense of worth must come from within.

And you can tell when you're needy because when people walk out of your life, you keep trying to talk them into staying. When you discover the power of focus, you will be secure within yourself and you will understand that sometimes God multiplies you by subtracting some things and some people from your life. Stop trying to convince people to stay in your life when they threaten to walk away. Let them go.

Stop worrying about stuff and about people whom the Lord is trying to deliver you from. "Do you" was once a popular phrase, meaning "do what's right for you."[25] You have to be yourself and stop trying to be what others want you to be, because that impulse will cause you to drift away from your center and lead you to do things you really shouldn't. Jesus is an excellent example of being true to His calling without fearing what others thought or said about Him.

Make Time for What Matters

Jesus modeled the relationship between being focused and knowing your purpose. Throughout Jesus' ministry, He often pulled away from the crowds for solitude and rest. Time and time again after healing, teaching, preaching, casting out devils, and performing miracles, He took some personal time away from the disciples. In fact, Luke wrote, "Jesus often withdrew to lonely places and prayed" (Luke 5:16 NIV). So, when Jesus said, "learn of Me," it was because He knew the importance of taking time to separate yourself and seek rest for your mind and body. Jesus' solitude and silence was a major theme in the Gospels and the key to His peace and His power.

You can't be the parent God wants you to be if you never take the time to invest in your own well-being. You can't be the teacher, the choir member, the usher, or the community advocate God wants you to be if you never make time for your own prayer life and time in the Word.

If people don't understand why you aren't available to them, that's their problem and not yours. If you want to get your energy and strength back, you've got to make up your mind about what matters and what doesn't. You are no longer going to be held down, held back, and held up by what "they" think, and what "they" say, or by what "they" are doing.

Life is a lot like sports in this regard. In sports, when the game is getting away from you, when the opponent is running up the score and it seems as if things are getting out of hand, a good coach or a good player knows when it's time to take a time out. Some of the most memorable losses in sports history occurred when players didn't know when to call a time out.

Here's what the Bible says in Philippians 4:7: "And the peace of God, which surpasses all understanding, will guard your hearts and your minds in Christ Jesus" (NRSV). Rather than worrying about "them," focus on the peace that comes from the God you serve. Let God's peace guard your heart and your mind so you can get your energy back.

In our culture of overworking and boasting in how busy we are, Jesus says, "I want to help you find peace, balance, and harmony." Over two thousand years ago, Jesus did that by pulling away from the crowds and the disciples, but today I think He would say you can find rest by pulling away from your cell phone and computer every now and then. Stop being so connected to email, text messages, and social media. Even when you are engaged in Kingdom activities, find time to unplug and take a break here and there so you can spend time on yourself, with your family, with a mentor, and especially with God in prayer.

Wayne Cordeiro said, "We won't be held accountable for how much we have done, but for how much we have done of what He has asked us to do."[26] When Jesus told the parable of the talents in Matthew 25:23, the master said, "Well done, good and faithful servant" (NIV). Those words were not about quantity, or how much he had done, but about quality—accomplishing what God wanted him to do. "You have been faithful with a few things; I will put you in charge of many things." At the end of your days, won't you want to hear the Lord say, *"Well done"*?

Chapter Five Questions

Question: How satisfied are you with the way you spend your time? What would you need to drop in order to do the things you really value in life or to fulfill the purpose God has shown you?

_____

_____

_____

_____

_____

_____

_____

_____

_____

Question: Do you find it easy to say no to people? Why? To what extent do your self-esteem and the image you seek to portray influence your choice of activities, possessions, and relationships?

_____

_____

_____

_____

_____

_____

_____

_____

_____

_____

Question: Jesus managed His time, despite the enormous pressures on Him, to rest and draw strength from the Father. What practical steps can you take to do the same?

_____

_____

_____

_____

_____

_____

Action: Do an energy audit to determine what is draining you, and then work out your return on investment in those areas. Are those activities worthwhile in terms of the benefit you receive? What needs to change to avoid burnout? Think of how you can spend more time on yourself and the people who matter most in your life.

Chapter Five Notes

_____

_____

_____

_____

_____

_____

_____

_____

_____

_____

_____

_____

_____

_____

_____

_____

_____

_____

_____

CHAPTER SIX

That's What Friends Are For

Friendship is important because, no matter who you are in life, you're going to need somebody. Someone to support you, someone to console you, someone to stand with and by you. God has created us to be social beings. You were never intended to try to make it through the ups and downs—the good times and the bad times that life sends your way—by yourself. You need people who care about you. And only time will teach you who your real friends are.

It seems like every generation struggles with its own weak substitutes for genuine friendship. And in an era of social media, where people have often replaced real relationships and authentic interaction with virtual contacts, likes, and online followers, the meaning and the value of true friendship is being lost in the shuffle. For some young people, friends have been replaced by Youtubers and social media influencers, whom they regard as mentors who really care about them.

But quite often these Youtubers and social media influencers are just enterprising entrepreneurs who have figured out how to make a profit out of giving their digital followers the illusion of friendship. In fact, authentic friendship is about mutual affection, trust, and the ability to be oneself without fear of judgment; ultimately, friendship is reciprocal, a two-way street, not just imitating the lifestyle, beliefs, and actions of someone on a screen who doesn't even know you.

To be clear, deprioritizing real friendship isn't just a problem for young people. I think one reason divorce is so high and so many relationships fall apart is because people don't prioritize being friends, and instead focus more on making a living than on liking one another. That's why I like the following text in Mark, because it is so pregnant with meaning about the power of friendship:

When [Jesus] returned to Capernaum after some days, it was reported that he was at home. So many gathered around that there was no longer room for them, not even in front of the door; and he was speaking the word to them. Then some people came, bringing to him a paralyzed man, carried by four of them. And when they could not bring him to Jesus because of the crowd, they removed the roof above him; and after having dug through it, they let down the mat on which the paralytic lay. When Jesus saw their faith, he said to the paralytic, "Son, your sins are forgiven." Now some of the scribes were sitting there, questioning in their hearts, "Why does this fellow speak in this way? It is blasphemy! Who can forgive sins but God alone?" At once Jesus perceived in his spirit that they were discussing these questions among themselves; and he said to them, "Why do you raise such questions in your hearts? Which is easier, to say to the paralytic, 'Your sins are forgiven,' or to say, 'Stand up and take your mat and walk'? But so that you may know that the Son of Man has authority on earth to forgive sins"—he said to the paralytic—"I say to you, stand up, take your mat and go to your home." And he stood up, and immediately took the mat and went out before all of them; so that they were all amazed and glorified God, saying, "We have never seen anything like this!"

—Mark 2:1–12 NRSV

We know that Jesus ministered to great crowds of people and healed all who came to Him for help. But what happened to those who couldn't get to Him? In this chapter, we will look more closely at this story of four enterprising men and their paralyzed friend.

Sacrificial Friendship

If you want to know whether a person in your life is a true friend, consider the actions of the four men in our text who brought their paralyzed friend to Jesus. The first sign of their friendship was their willingness to make personal sacrifices.

As Jesus returned home, word circulated that He was back in town. According to Mark chapter 1, Jesus had already been healing many people. He healed Simon's mother-in-law of a fever, drove out demons from those who were possessed, and cured a man with leprosy, as well as many others. By Mark chapter 2, Jesus' reputation as a healer, a man sent from God, had already spread. And so, the house where He was teaching was packed, because people saw in Jesus the potential to get something that they needed or wanted for themselves. They were thinking, "If Jesus did all those things for those people, then perhaps He can do something for me."

I'm sure the four men in this text had issues of their own: financial problems, family issues, and their own physical challenges. Without their friend, they could have pushed their way in and received help. Yet this journey of friendship was made possible because the four men were more focused on their friend's needs than on themselves, what they could get, or how they could benefit from the revival service. And a sign of a true friend is someone who is willing to put your needs above their own.

Maybe they supported him during his time of need because he had supported them at some point in the past. Nothing impedes a friendship more than a person who makes it all about himself or herself. But when people aren't selfish, it's not a chore to help them. These men understood the responsibility that comes with friendship. Quality relationships require a commitment and come at a cost, and true friends are those who understand that a relationship requires you to give of yourself sometimes. Be careful of linking up with people who only want to take from you and never sacrifice or give anything back to you.

The Test of Loyalty

Secondly, they were willing to stand by him when he was down. The text does not tell us how long the man had been paralyzed. Several other miracle accounts or healing episodes offer details about a person being lame or blind from birth, but here we do not get an indication that the man was a lifelong paralytic. It is possible that at one time, he'd been able to walk. His relationship with these guys probably included a time when they were able to do things together. But now, maybe as the result of an accident, the man was paralyzed. He was no longer able to work, earn a living, or pay his way as he once did. He had fallen on hard times, and yet his friends still stuck by him. They didn't allow his circumstances to influence their relationship. You really know who your true friends are not by where they stand when you're riding high, but by where they stand when you fall on hard times.

Faith in Action

Thirdly, along with making personal sacrifices and providing support, the friends weren't deterred by the obstacles they faced together. Just picture the difficulties in getting this man to Jesus. There was the physical impossibility of entering the house. There was the attitude of other people who saw him and refused to give him access. There was his own pride and embarrassment to overcome, and maybe even a lack of belief since the text only mentions their faith, not his. Then there were the religious leaders, a watchful and hostile element who opposed what Jesus was doing.

Let's consider for a moment the crowds who were blocking the entrance. These people were willing to step over the man in need in order to hear Jesus talking about helping people in need! What a sad commentary that their desire to hear Jesus never translated into wanting to create space for those who needed Him. Here they were soaking up the words of Jesus for themselves while blocking those who needed a touch from the Master.

How eerily similar to today, when so-called Christian people have a self-centered preoccupation that causes them to drive by, step over, and overlook the very ones Jesus is trying to help. We have a society today filled with religious gluttons who get satiated on the teachings of Jesus but never put his teachings into practice. We buy books about Jesus, attend conferences about Jesus, and listen to religious podcasts and songs about Him, but we rarely devote ourselves to helping the people Jesus came to help. It's all about self. We've become hearers of the Word but not doers.

Like the crowds in that house, the struggle in the world today is with church folk who think the focus should be on them rather than on the needs of others. But these men showed their loyalty to their friend by their willingness to separate from the crowds to stay connected with him. The text makes it clear that the who's who of Capernaum were in attendance on that day, but not one of these men abandoned him so they could get access for themselves. The mark of genuine connection is not determined by how you are treated when you are in the room, but rather by who sticks with you when you can't get in.

Dealing with Discouragement

When we hear Jesus say to the man, "Your sins are forgiven," we tend to think that the man is guilty of some moral flaw that resulted in him being paralyzed. But the Greek word translated as *sin* merely means to miss, or fail to hit, the mark.[27] It is possible that the shortcomings hinted at in the text were not moral, but psychological, having less to do with what caused him to become paralyzed and more to do with the impact paralysis had on his state of mind.

Most of us would struggle to adjust to such a drastic change in our lives. Everything he once had was gone; he couldn't earn a living, and people ignored or insulted him every day. After being paralyzed for a while, maybe this formerly vibrant man had allowed his outer condition to affect his inner disposition. He had started to internalize his situation, saw all those people look him over, and became discouraged.

Before Jesus could speak to the man's external inability to walk, He had to speak to the internal problem, the state of his mind. To heal the man's legs without fixing the condition of his psyche would have given him the power to walk without the courage to go somewhere. So Jesus spoke to his inner discouragement, which was preventing him from walking into his future. Jesus wanted to release him from the depression that had set in.

Maybe you need to hear Jesus say your sins are forgiven—that you no longer have to hold on to the disappointment that comes with failure or the discouragement that comes from your situation. The onset of depression affected another paralyzed man in Scripture. In John 5, the man sat by a pool for thirty-eight years; it was a pool of potential healing, yet his opportunity was intercepted by people faster than he was. The man was so preoccupied with others that he constantly missed what he needed, but Jesus raised the question, "Do you want to be made well?" (John 5:6 NRSV). Friends help you push through psychological barriers.

They also help you overcome systemic barriers. The text says there were religious leaders present in the house who were more preoccupied with questioning Jesus than helping people. They were more concerned with defending a particular religious system and set of doctrines that upheld the social order than with helping a man in need. They were like those today who want to argue about baptismal formulas and doctrinal creeds but ignore public policies that paralyze and cripple communities. They will debate you about the name in which you were baptized and whether you speak in tongues, but they can't even witness to their neighbor in desperate need.

Theirs is a faith that is cold and anemic. True religion operates not only on the vertical plane but also on the horizontal—it seeks not only to integrate men with God but to connect the various members of the human family with one another. While the man was in need of healing, the religious folk were caught up defending the system.

Thank God that what the man could not get from the crowd or the religious leaders, he could get from his friends. Because his friends understood that unjust systems don't deserve to stand. Instead of giving up in the face of opposition, they had to remind their friend and themselves that they were closer than ever to healing.

Going the Extra Mile

Despite the crowds, despite the self-esteem issues, and despite the systemic impediments, the men were willing to go the extra mile and take their friend to the roof. I think they did that because they saw something in him that perhaps he didn't even see in himself. Your friends see purpose and potential in you, even when you're down on your luck, that you may not even see in yourself. His friends were willing to go the extra mile because his situation didn't define his destination; his position didn't determine his potential.

He was severely disabled, but he was still their friend. And so, even though the door where Jesus was teaching was blocked by the crowd, they said to themselves, "If we can't get him in the door, we can take him through the roof." They did not allow their friend to park his pursuit at the door of limitation.

Real friendship pushes you past your limits. They raised him to the roof because increasing his elevation lifted him above his obstacles. They entered on the ground level, but the blessing came by their willingness to take him higher. Real friends are willing to elevate you when life seeks to relegate you. Some people never get the healing they need because of their refusal to be raised higher than where they currently are.

When they got there, the men encountered another obstacle. It was a clay roof, but that was okay. They didn't let the clay stand in their way, either. They started digging through the roof, and as the pieces of dirt began falling on those below, the obstacle intended to block them ended up blessing them. It was the particles of dirt from the roof that got Jesus' attention—because they had torn through the thing that was blocking the possibility of a better life.

These men were willing to do whatever it took, even if it meant getting dirty, to see their friend get the break-through he needed. Anyone can be loyal when the circumstances of your life are clean and free from stain, but a real friend sticks with you in the midst of the dirty realities of life.

And because of their determination to help their friend and stand by his side, Jesus looked beyond the disruption of his message and saw their faith. The text says that when he saw "their faith," Jesus spoke a word of freedom, lib-eration, healing, and purpose. This man got healed, he got blessed, and he got delivered not because of anything he had done but because of whom he was connected to.

The Power of Connection

I remember preaching in Jersey years ago for a friend, and after the revival, I was looking forward to eating at this soul food restaurant. When the service was over, it was around 9 p.m. The restaurant didn't close until 10, so I was excited; we still had time to get there. After chang-ing my clothes, I was waiting in the pastor's study, but he was taking forever to come in so we could leave. I learned it was because a lady in the service said she had an emer-gency and wanted to talk to him. While the issue was of extreme importance, selfishly, I looked at my watch. It was now 9:35, and I was getting kind of concerned. I went back into the sanctuary to see if I could urge the pastor to move it along.

He must have seen my facial expression, so he had one of his leaders rush me out and take me to the restaurant.

When we pulled up, it was 9:59, and an employee was locking up and turning off the light. She had just turned the "open" sign around to "closed." I was disappointed and returned to the car.

After I'd gotten back in the car, the employee knocked on the window and asked, "Sir, are you a friend of Pastor Jefferson?" I said yes. She said, "I was told to reopen the restaurant because your friend knows the owner." Then she explained that she was going to serve me because of my relationship with the pastor, my friend.

When you are walking with God, He loves to bless you both directly and indirectly, through other people. Expect some blessings not because of anything you've done but because of your connections. That's what friends are for—to give and receive spiritual blessings through earthly means. All of us are to be like the four men in this text; we are called to be barrier removers. Isn't that what God does for us?

What's more, if human beings are prepared to go to these lengths, why wouldn't a loving, merciful Father go even further? Yet some of us are slow to believe in God's kindness. Even if we believe it, we're not always willing to pass on that love to others.

Jesus described those who would be welcomed into His kingdom, saying of them:

"For I was hungry and you gave me something to eat, I was thirsty and you gave me something to drink, I was a stranger and you invited me in, I needed clothes and you clothed me, I was sick and you looked after me, I was in prison and you came to visit me."

> *Then the righteous will answer him, "Lord, when did we*
> *see you hungry and feed you, or thirsty and give you some-*
> *thing to drink? When did we see you a stranger and invite*
> *you in, or needing clothes and clothe you? When did we see*
> *you sick or in prison and go to visit you?"*
>
> *The King will reply, "Truly I tell you, whatever you did for*
> *one of the least of these brothers and sisters of mine, you*
> *did for me."*
>
> **—Matthew 25:35–40** NIV

You can't be a friend of God and an enemy of people. You cannot be comfortable in your church groups while there are people on the margins of society without access to the help and resources they need. The men in the text did it because they were the man's friends, but you must do it as an ambassador of Christ.

WORKBOOK

Chapter Six Questions

Question: The house where Jesus was preaching was so full, the men couldn't even get in the door. Who or what might be blocking you from drawing close to Jesus? What extremes would you go to in order to get closer?

_____

_____

_____

_____

_____

_____

_____

_____

_____

_____

Question: Jesus made a point of telling the man he was forgiven before He told him to get up and walk. Why do you think this was important? How do sin, guilt, and discouragement affect your daily walk with God?

_____

_____

_____

_____

_____

_____

_____

_____

_____

_____

Question: What are you doing as an ambassador of Christ to help those most in need? What more could you do? What holds you back?

_____

_____

_____

_____

_____

_____

_____

_____

_____

_____

Action: This chapter makes it clear that friendship means more than a social connection—it's about commitment and sacrifice. How will you demonstrate that kind of support to your friends, family, coworkers, and other contacts?

Chapter Six Notes

CHAPTER SEVEN

Seize the Day

You have probably heard of the Latin phrase *carpe diem,* which means, "seize the day."[28] The Roman poet Horace used it in a longer sentence, translated as: "pluck the day, trusting as little as possible in the next one."[29] The idea is that the future is unknown, so don't wait to do tomorrow what you can do today.

Jesus conveyed similar thoughts when He said, "So do not worry about tomorrow, for tomorrow will bring worries of its own. Today's trouble is enough for today" (Matthew 6:34 NRSV). The point is to never allow your hopes to be extinguished or your progress halted by the perils of the past or the anxieties of the future.

Seize the day. Take hold of the possibilities that lie before you instead of allowing what happened behind you to incarcerate you. Don't allow fear, doubt, and regret to keep you from doing, getting, and possessing all that God has in store for you!

Strength in Suffering

The Gospels recount the story of a brave woman with a hidden disease who broke social and religious taboos to seize the day and draw close to Jesus for healing.

And a woman was there who had been subject to bleeding for twelve years. She had suffered a great deal under the care of many doctors and had spent all she had, yet instead of getting better she grew worse. When she heard about Jesus, she came up behind him in the crowd and touched his cloak, because she thought, "If I just touch his clothes, I will be healed." Immediately her bleeding stopped and she felt in her body that she was freed from her suffering.

At once Jesus realized that power had gone out from him. He turned around in the crowd and asked, "Who touched my clothes?"

"You see the people crowding against you," his disciples answered, "and yet you can ask, 'Who touched me?'"

But Jesus kept looking around to see who had done it. Then the woman, knowing what had happened to her, came and fell at his feet and, trembling with fear, told him the whole truth. He said to her, "Daughter, your faith has healed you. Go in peace and be freed from your suffering."
—Mark 5:25–34 NIV

No one better typifies fortitude in the face of suffering and seemingly insurmountable difficulty than the woman with an issue of blood in the preceding text. We don't know her name, but we are given access to her struggle. Perhaps the reason why no doctor was able to heal her was because they were treating her symptoms and not the cause.

A while ago, I was staying at a hotel. I turned up the heat but noticed it was still cold. I called the front desk, and they said they could bring me a space heater or a blanket, or move my room to another side of the hotel. When I asked why they offered all these little things instead of turning the heat up in the room, they replied, "The system is broken." It hit me that they were trying to function by providing small solutions to a much deeper problem. Don't give me a space heater—fix the system. Don't give me a blanket—fix the system.

What I like about this woman in the text is that she did not allow her condition to snuff out her determination to find real, deep healing. She pressed her way through the crowd and touched Jesus. She seized her opportunity; she seized her moment. She seized the day.

Mother Teresa said, "Yesterday is gone and tomorrow has not yet come; we must live each day as if it were our last...."[30] Ralph Waldo Emerson said, "Write it on your heart that every day is the best day in the year."[31] The apostle Paul put it this way in his letter to the Philippians:

> *Beloved, I do not consider that I have made it my own; but this one thing I do: forgetting what lies behind and straining forward to what lies ahead, I press on toward the goal for the prize of the heavenly call of God in Christ Jesus.*
> *—Philippians 3:13–14 NRSV*

The Bible says that this woman seized her opportunity, and when she did that, she was healed in an instant. How amazing! This woman could have given up; she could have thrown in the towel on herself, on God, and on her future, but she didn't. She marshaled the strength she had left to pursue the desired outcome. Rather than allowing her past disappointments to hinder her, she took advantage of the opportunity she had. When she heard that Jesus—the healer, the miracle worker—was in the vicinity, she took the risk of faith to pursue her healing.

Learning to Endure

Just imagine what this woman had been through. Over twelve years, she had to learn to endure. Mark 5:26 says that "she had endured much" (NRSV). Endurance is the capacity to go through something and not let it get the best of you. What inspires me, and what I hope inspires you, about this woman is that she did not allow her pain or her disappointment to get the best of her. For twelve years, she endured this blood issue. That's 144 months, 624 weeks, 4,383 days, or over 105,000 hours. And after all that, she did not fall apart when the thing she wanted did not work out the way she desired. The Bible says she had suffered many things by many doctors and yet, rather than her condition getting better, it got worse.

Yet it appears that the deterioration of her condition did not translate into the destruction of her faith. Her condition might have gotten worse, but her faith got stronger. Twelve years is a long time to have to deal with a problem. It's a long time to be sick, heartbroken, unemployed, or trapped in an unproductive space. Some people can't handle a challenge for twelve days, let alone twelve years. Long-term suffering can wear you down and wear you out. You would think that after twelve years, she would have given up, concluding it wasn't going to happen. But she didn't do that. Instead, she made the most of it by not allowing the setback to hold her back. She decided that what didn't kill her could be used to make her stronger. Sometimes God does not deliver you from your trials right away, but He preserves you in your trials and gives you the power to endure.

Don't miss the real power of the text. The blood is symbolic of life. For twelve years, she was losing life, but in those twelve years, she never lost her life. She was not free from her problems, but she also was not destroyed by them. Is that not the story of Daniel in the lions' den (Daniel 6)? God kept him in the den, but He rendered the lions impotent. He didn't bring immediate deliverance *from* the den but enabled endurance *in* the den.

Look at the three Hebrew boys (Shadrach, Meshach and Abednego), Daniel's friends, who were thrown into a blazing furnace for refusing to worship the king (Daniel 3). They were not delivered from the fire initially. In fact, the fire was said to have been made several times hotter. But instead of freeing them from the fire, God made them fireproof.

God may not free you from your struggle, but He will preserve you in it. He'll preserve your power, your peace, and your patience. God allowed Satan to take everything Job had, but the enemy couldn't take his life—and through his terrible distress, Job came into a deeper relationship with God (Job 42:5). This woman with the issue of blood was learning the same way. She seized the moment by understanding that her issues did not control, delimit, or define her. She endured the suffering and met Jesus.

This is reminiscent of what the apostle James wrote to the persecuted church: "My brothers and sisters, whenever you face trials of any kind, consider it nothing but joy, because you know that the testing of your faith produces endurance" (James 1:2–3 NRSV).

Mark's gospel account reveals something I think was key to helping her endure: she endured because she listened to the right things. After spending all she had on doctors who used her for her money and still didn't help her, Mark said, "she had heard about Jesus" (Mark 5:27 NRSV). When she heard about Jesus, she wanted to get close, and pressed her way through the crowd. Rather than listening to the negative and giving up, she chose to listen to the positive. Oftentimes, we listen to the wrong things, the wrong people, the wrong stats, or the wrong facts.

Failure hurts, but sometimes it's necessary to help you find the answer you need.

Knocking on the Right Door

There was a further difficulty facing this woman. The Levitical law, the law of the temple, labeled her as unclean because of her illness; she shouldn't even be mixing in society (Leviticus 15). So, not only did she have this issue, but there was also social and religious stigma associated with her situation. How tragic for religious folks to ostracize her because of her condition! She was in a crowd of people listening to Jesus, but they made no place for her personhood, her pain, or her predicament.

And yet, after all that, she didn't allow the religious restrictions of others to keep her from getting the blessing she needed. She heard about Jesus, and in so doing, she had her ear attuned to the positive rather than the negative. What are you listening to, as you endure your own situa tion? What you allow into your ears, your heart, and your spirit really does matter. The Bible says faith comes by hearing, and hearing by the word of God (Romans 10:17).

Nothing breaks down one's endurance faster than internalizing the negativity and toxicity of other people. You should become allergic to negative people and immune to their remarks. Learn to endure by listening to what God says about you, not what people say to you. People may say you're a failure, that you won't make it and you should give up. But don't hear it. I like this woman because she never internalized the defeat. She didn't allow what had happened and what others said to keep her down; she kept getting back up.

To do that, you must be persistent. I appreciate the sense that this woman had to push and press her way through the crowd. Perhaps what enabled her to do so is found in something that the Gospel of Mark tells us, which the Gospel of Luke doesn't capture in his account. Mark wrote that when she heard about Jesus, she said to herself, "If I but touch his clothes, I will be made well" (Mark 5:8 NRSV). This woman pressed past the crowd by talking to herself, convincing herself to do something that was a risk. Both Gospels suggest that the woman was afraid when she came. But she talked her way past her fears.

I like that she talked to herself. Just like you have to be careful whom you listen to, you have to be careful whom

112 · DELMAN COATES

you talk to. She did not give others the chance to talk her out of her opportunity.

There are times in life when you can't wait to be encouraged or affirmed by others; you have to affirm your own self-worth. There are times when you have to encourage yourself. As Donald Lawrence's song "Encourage Yourself" says, "Sometimes you have to speak the word over yourself. The pressure is all around, but God is present help. The enemy created walls, but remember giants, they do fall."[32]

The woman with the issue of blood could not press on if she allowed the thoughts, opinions, and ideas of other people to incarcerate her. If you're going to seize the day, you can't get caught up in listening or talking to the crowd. This woman made up her mind she was going to do whatever it took. She had come too far to quit, working too long and fighting too hard to throw in the towel. She would rather have died trying than remain alive by giving up.

We know this woman today because she didn't quit. I can see her saying to herself, "Today is going to be the day of my miracle. Today is going to be the day when my situation is going to turn around." Despite all she had endured in the past, she still believed that this day could be the day she was healed. This woman rejected the idea that her issue was permanent. It wasn't until she ran out of her own resources that she ran into Jesus. After twelve years of suffering, humiliation, and a host of different treatments, she seized her opportunity.

To paraphrase a saying commonly attributed to Thomas A. Edison, many of life's failures are a result of people not realizing how close they were to success when they gave up. What doctors could not do in years, Jesus did within seconds. The woman's problem was, she kept trying the wrong people. She had been knocking on the wrong doors, but that day she came to the right Person and got all the help she needed.

Taking the Risk

Most people who discuss this text talk about the power of the woman touching the hem of Jesus' garment, but before she could touch him, she had to *reach*. The woman with the issue of blood didn't know if it would work, but faith prompted her to reach out to Jesus even when she didn't have all the answers. That confirms what the Bible says: "Now faith is the substance of things hoped for, the evidence of things not seen" (Hebrews 11:1 NKJV). The faith necessary to seize the moment does not always come with all the answers. It's oftentimes unclear. You don't see the full picture.

It was not enough just to show up. If she was going to be healed, she had to take action. She could not just wait on God; she had to do something. Jesus had the power, but she had to take the risk. It was a big risk, because the law said that not only was she unclean but anyone she touched would become unclean, too. Taking the risk is a divine–human partnership that matches our faith and action with God's power and willingness.

The apostle James said that faith without action is dead (James 2:17). We ought to pray like it's all up to God but work like it's all up to us. Somewhere between prayer and works, something starts to happen. The Bible says she reached *and* she touched. The healing was just as much in the reach as it was in the touch. In fact, there was no healing touch without a human reach.

You have to do the reaching if you want God to do the healing. Despite her weakness, the woman maintained her desire to reach after something. Dr. Benjamin E. Mays, former president of Morehouse College said, "It must be borne in mind that the tragedy of life doesn't lie in not reaching your goal. The tragedy lies in having no goal to reach. It isn't a calamity to die with dreams unfulfilled, but it is a calamity not to dream. It is not a disaster to be unable to capture your ideal but it is a disaster to have no ideal to capture. It is not a disgrace not to reach the stars, but it is a disgrace to have no stars to reach for. Not failure, but low aim, is sin."[33] The woman reached, and it worked. The Bible says that her flow of blood immediately stopped!

After all that time, after all that struggle, she got what she needed—she got to the root cause of the problem. First, her physical condition got better, but down in verse 34, she received more. She was made whole and granted peace. Being healed addressed her sickness in her body, but being whole freed her. Jesus corrected all the other problems that her sickness had created. Being made whole means nothing is missing; nothing is lacking. When you take the risk, Jesus makes you whole.

WORKBOOK

Chapter Seven Questions

Question: The woman had endured long years of suffering but found the courage to reach out to Jesus. Who are you most likely to reach out to, when you are struggling? Do you find it difficult to turn to God instead of seeking human solutions?

_____

_____

_____

_____

_____

_____

_____

_____

_____

Question: The woman told herself that Jesus would heal her. Have you ever spoken words of affirmation over yourself? To what extent do the voices around you and the opinions of others influence you when you're going through hardship?

_____

_____

_____

_____

_____

_____

_____

_____

_____

Question: Jesus was on His way to save a dying child when He felt the power go out of Him. Why do you think it was so important to stop and find out who had touched Him? What does that say about how He balanced time pressures against human need?

_____

_____

_____

_____

_____

_____

_____

_____

_____

_____

Action: Being faithful and steadfast in times of trouble can be hard, but the Bible tells us we also need to put our faith into action. In what areas can you exercise patience and move forward in faith as you wait on God for deliverance?

Chapter Seven Notes

_____

_____

_____

_____

_____

_____

_____

_____

_____

_____

_____

_____

_____

_____

_____

_____

_____

_____

CHAPTER EIGHT

God Will Handle Your Haters

The popular TV show *Game of Thrones* was about an array of rulers, kingdoms, and dynasties all vying for power, including the right to sit in the highest position of authority in the land, called the Iron Throne.[34] It was a grim tale of brutal conflict and treachery, as well as unlikely alliances and the struggle for survival. I think what drew the audience to this show was the drama around knowing who is for you and who is against you—and seeing how people, if you aren't careful, will stab you in the back.

One of the many things I have learned from watching *Game of Thrones* is that success in life comes when you are clear about who your enemy is and you know how to defeat them. We prefer to navigate through life without conflict and to avoid rivals, adversaries, and foes. We prefer things to be smooth and easy, instead of having to overcome obstacles and hindrances. But *Game of Thrones* forces people to confront the very thing we would prefer to avoid: the reality that opposition, resistance, and challenges are a fact of life.

King David was a man with a lot of enemies. He knew what it was to be surrounded and powerless, completely dependent on God's protection. He wrote Psalm 59 as a cry for help:

Deliver me from my enemies, O God; be my fortress against those who are attacking me. Deliver me from evildoers and save me from those who are after my blood.

See how they lie in wait for me! Fierce men conspire against me for no offense or sin of mine, LORD. I have done no wrong, yet they are ready to attack me. Arise to help me; look on my plight! You, LORD God Almighty, you who are the God of Israel, rouse yourself to punish all the nations; show no mercy to wicked traitors.

They return at evening, snarling like dogs, and prowl about the city. See what they spew from their mouths—the words from their lips are sharp as swords, and they think, "Who can hear us?" But you laugh at them, LORD; you scoff at all those nations.

You are my strength, I watch for you; you, God, are my fortress, my God on whom I can rely.

God will go before me and will let me gloat over those who slander me.
                                    —Psalm 59:1–10 NIV

For people of faith, it's important to know you will have struggles. You will have enemies—people maneuvering and plotting to get where you are, to take what you have and to move you aside. It is quite possible that if you don't have any enemies, it's because you haven't been standing for anything.

Victor Hugo said, "You have enemies? Why, it is the story of every man who has done a great deed or created a new idea. It is the cloud which thunders around everything which shines."[35] They are a sign we're doing something right. Leadership expert Robert Greene says, "If you have no enemies, find a way to make them."[36] Whenever you are doing the right thing, doing what God wants you to do and standing on the principles of God's Word, you will have haters and you will face opposition.

David and the Haters

Now, before I go further, let me define *hater*. A hater is not someone who doesn't like you because you're mean or because you treat people wrong. People who are hurt by you are not the same as people who are hating on you for no apparent reason. I note that, because some people use the idea of haters to defend being arrogant, cruel, and flat-out nasty.

But by *hater* I mean someone who doesn't like you because of the God you serve, the values you espouse, and the principles upon which you stand. A hater is someone who doesn't like the God in you and will do whatever they can to stop, block, or frustrate the assignment God has given you. You can have them in your job, in your circle, in your family, and in your church; sometimes, you can have haters in your own house. They try to crush your dreams and aspirations, to keep you from your destiny.

They try to stop your progress because, really, they are insecure with themselves.

If you live long enough, there will be people who try to obstruct you, situations that will challenge you, and obstacles that will discourage you. Psalm 59 reveals that opposition accompanies anointing and lets you know that salvation doesn't make you immune to it.

When David was still a shepherd boy, God sent His prophet Samuel to anoint David as king (1 Samuel 16). Yet despite this personal appointment, David still had to deal with powerful opposition. Years of disappointment followed at the hands of other people who wanted to hinder his progress, obstruct his future, and block his blessings, even after he was finally crowned king.

David was a warrior, but also a man of faith who knew how to worship God in the face of his haters. As a boy, he was despised in his own household and forced to work the fields alone. While doing his job as a shepherd, he was threatened by lions and bears who rose up against him and attacked his sheep. Then, as a teenager, he went into battle against a Philistine giant named Goliath who had attacked God's people.

And each time, David was given the victory—whether the opposition came from without or within, whether it was the lions, the bears, or a giant. God gave David victory over his haters.

Not surprisingly, he often found himself dealing with opposition from Saul, the very king God chose him to succeed. By the time we get to Psalm 59, David had been on the run from King Saul for some time. The David who wrote Psalm 59 was not the confident David of Psalm 27 who declared: "The LORD is my light and my salvation; whom shall I fear? The LORD is the strength of my life; of whom shall I be afraid?" (Psalm 27:1 NKJV). The David who wrote Psalm 59 was living in darkness, weakened and afraid for his life. David had haters everywhere he went. He couldn't even set foot outside his house because Saul's men were watching and had orders to kill him. Yet, in the midst of this, David penned Psalm 59 to remind you that if you let Him, God will handle your haters.

Maybe you are in a job where you are stressed out and mistreated, mismanaged by a boss who doesn't like you and undermined by coworkers who can't stand you. Whatever your situation, no matter how many are standing against you, God will handle your haters.

A Mighty Fortress

So, how does God do it, you might ask? Well, first, according to the text, God plays defense on your behalf.

Paul "Bear" Bryant once said that "defense wins championships."[37] The Detroit Pistons of the early 2000s were a ragtag team that knocked off the three-time championship Los Angeles Lakers, in part because of their strong defensive skills.[38] They didn't have a superstar on their team, but they all showed up each game and played defense.

It's not just true on the sports field; it's also true in the game of life. If you want to be great, if you want to go to the next level, you have to be able to trust God to have your back. David said God loves you so much that when enemies attack you, He's willing to play defense for you. It's what God does.

David said in the very first verse of Psalm 59, "Deliver me from my enemies, O God; be my fortress against those who are attacking me" (NIV). Throughout the Psalms, and elsewhere in Scripture, references to the architecture of the battlefield are quite common. God is often described as a shield, a horn, a high tower, a stronghold, and a rock of safety. By using this imagery, the warrior David said God can handle your haters by moving you out of their reach. That's the good news of the text—that God plays defense.

There are many times when Scripture tells us we don't need to fear our enemies. For example, Moses told the Israelites when they were about to enter the Promised Land, "Be strong and courageous. Do not be afraid or terrified because of them, for the LORD your God goes with you; he will never leave you nor forsake you" (Deuteronomy 31:6 NIV).

As James Cleveland sang, "If I hold my peace, let the Lord fight my battles; I know that the victory shall be mine."[39]

A Strong Deliverer

Not only does God play defense, but He also provides deliverance. God will defend you when haters attack you, and He'll deliver you from them. David called to God for deliverance twice in the first few verses of Psalm 59. In verse 1, he asked God to deliver him from his enemies, while in verse 2, he asked God to deliver him from evildoers and save him from those who were after his blood. Like God's defensive posture, deliverance figures prominently in the Psalms. In fact, throughout Scripture, we read accounts of how God saved His people from dangerous situations, often in miraculous ways—like the Israelites escaping slavery in Egypt, Daniel in the lions' den, and Peter being busted from prison by an angel.

When I think about God's deliverance, I think of Him like the big brother in a video clip I once saw. He ran into a wrestling match where his sister was not doing so well against her opponent. The big brother jumped on her opponent, pushed him out of the way, and yelled, "Get off my sister!" He stepped onto the mat to defend his sister and delivered her from the defeat she was about to encounter.

That's what God does. He steps in to deliver you. He gets in the ring with you to free you from your foes and deliver you from your enemies. Regardless of who you are and what you're going through in life, God is a deliverer. In another psalm, David said it like this: "You prepare a table before me in the presence of my enemies; you anoint my head with oil; my cup overflows" (Psalm 23:5 NRSV). In the face of your oppressors, in the depth of your situation, God's anointing gives you deliverance from your enemies!

Working Out in God's Gym

God not only plays defense and provides deliverance, but He also handles your haters by promoting your development. It is the spiritually immature person who despairs in the face of adversity; the mature saint understands that adversity comes not to defeat you but to develop you.

I observed something interesting one day at the gym. I saw a man come in to obtain membership and exercise, and everything about what he was wearing said that he had come in for a serious workout. He wore the typical attire: matching t-shirt and shorts, some kind of waist belt, a water bottle, and weightlifting gloves. I saw him stretching like he was really about to go after it. Then he went to the area where the weights were, grabbed a few dumbbells, walked over to a bench, and sat down.

After doing a few bicep curls, he put the weights down and wiped off his forehead like he had really been doing something. In an exasperated voice, he said, "Whoof! That's enough for me today!" After that, he got dressed and left. That was it! He looked the part, but he didn't really come to the gym for a workout.

That's how many Christians act when we go to church. We look like we are ready for a workout. We wear the right clothes, sing the right songs, and talk the right talk, but stop short of building real strength that requires effort and hard work. So sometimes, since we don't always take God's gym seriously, He brings His gym to us. Adverse circumstances are where He starts the training; standing firm in difficulty and navigating opposition is how He develops our spiritual muscles and makes us stronger.

Only a mature man could say, as David does in Psalm 23:5, "You prepare a table before me in the presence of my enemies" (NRSV). Only a faithful man like James could say, "Consider it nothing but joy, because you know that the testing of your faith produces endurance" (James 1:2b–3 NRSV). Struggles, opposition, and haters aren't always there to block you; sometimes, they are uniquely positioned to bless you.

The season of distress that David was going through in Psalm 59 taught him that oftentimes, God promotes in the midst of pain. God uses the circumstances of your life to shape you, mold you, and fashion you after His will and for His purposes. That's why the author of Psalm 119, also believed to be David, could say, "It was good for me to be afflicted so that I might learn your decrees" (Psalm 119:71 NIV).

Did you notice that the first eight verses in Psalm 59 are a complaint about the enemy David faced? But when we get to verse 9, there's a shift—from a man who was complaining about his trials to a man who was confident in the face of them and saw in them an opportunity to mature and grow. Listen to the language of verse 9: "You are my strength, I watch for you; you, God, are my fortress" (NIV).

This is not the same language of the scared man from verse 1. This is a faithful man who knows that despite what is happening around him, God still has a purpose for him. Between verse 1 and verse 9, there is growth, from a man who shrinks in the face of adversity and opposition to a man who stands in the face of it. And the key to success in life is realizing that every now and then, you have to matriculate through God's university of adversity if you are going to survive and grow.

A good illustration of this is a story about some farmers who became fed up with an old donkey that roamed the countryside chasing cows and chickens. In anger, they decided to get rid of the donkey by throwing him in an abandoned well and burying him with dirt and sand. When they began throwing dirt in the well, an amazing thing happened: as the dirt hit the donkey's back, he just shook it off and packed the dirt under his feet. They kept throwing dirt all day and all night, and as the donkey continued to repeat this, he kept rising until he had enough dirt under his feet to climb out of the well and walk away.

When your enemies throw dirt on you, have the sense of that donkey. Shake it off, pack it under your feet, and keep moving higher. Use the dirt to rise above your enemies and walk away victoriously.

The Justice of God

God handles your haters by playing defense, providing deliverance, and promoting your development. Lastly, God handles your haters by providing you with His divine justice. This is something difficult to fathom. It is an idea that lives at the limits of human reasoning and understanding. The French philosopher and mathematician Blaise Pascal said, "The finite is annihilated in the presence of the infinite, and becomes a pure nothing. So our spirit before God, so our justice before divine justice."[40] That's just another way of saying what the prophet Isaiah said:

"For my thoughts are not your thoughts, neither are your ways my ways," declares the LORD. "As the heavens are

higher than the earth, so are my ways higher than your
ways and my thoughts than your thoughts."
                        —Isaiah 55:8–9 NIV

And God's ways include His divine justice. Where is divine justice in Psalm 59? We know David wrote it when King Saul's men were surrounding his house, with direct orders from the king to kill him, and it is a prayer for God to handle his haters and enemies.

This scenario may seem strange given that David had at least one opportunity to take justice into his own hands and kill Saul. The Bible tells us in 1 Samuel 24 that when Saul heard David was near him, he took three companies, the best he could find in all Israel, and set out in search of David and his men. Then, in a cave, David had a chance to kill Saul. His men thought this was their opportunity to put an end to the powerful enemy who was standing in the way of David becoming king as God had promised. But rather than kill Saul, David quietly crept up behind him and cut off a piece of his robe, telling his men they should not lift a finger against God's anointed.

So, why did David not kill Saul when God had seemingly delivered him into David's hands? Why didn't the Lord instruct David to do so? I believe it was because God had justice awaiting Saul that David could not deliver. Not that David wasn't strong, but God was stronger. It's not that David's justice wasn't swift; God's was swifter. And I believe that David could hold his peace in 1 Samuel 24, and pray to keep his peace in Psalm 59, because he was assured of God's justice.

God's justice covers what we can't; it is strong enough to contend with the forces of evil all around us. God's justice makes little sense to us, but in the grand scheme of things, from God's vantage point, it always makes perfect sense. Divine justice is when you have been wronged or harmed but you trust God to work things out for you—moving people, removing obstacles, opening doors, and enlarging your territory. Divine justice is when the enemy means something for evil but God turns it around for your good.

It was this divine justice that Dr. King called "the arc of the moral universe." It "is long," King said, "but it bends toward justice."[41] That divine justice came in the form of a human being to avenge us against the wicked one, freeing us from the penalty and punishment of sin. Divine justice came through forty-two generations to be born in a manger on the wrong side of the tracks. Divine justice preached a gospel of justice for the poor and liberty to the captives. Divine justice was hanged high and stretched wide on an old rugged cross so that sin could not win—the grave robbed of victory and death of its sting.

WORKBOOK

Chapter Eight Questions

Question: Are you choosing to work out in God's gym, building spiritual strength and maturity, or are you choosing to struggle through the university of adversity? What are you learning? Is there more you could be doing?

_____

_____

_____

_____

_____

_____

_____

_____

_____

_____

Question: David often used battlefield terms to describe God as a place of refuge and safety. In what ways have you found God to be a shelter from the storms of life? What happens if you leave that safe place?

_____

_____

_____

_____

_____

_____

_____

_____

_____

_____

Question: What instances can you think of when you have experienced God's justice in turning around a bad situation? How does that compare with taking justice into your own hands?

_____

_____

_____

_____

_____

_____

_____

_____

_____

_____

_____

Action: God specializes in defense and deliverance on our behalf. What battles are you fighting that you could leave for Him to sort out? What will you do to give Him the space and time to act?

Chapter Eight Notes

_____

_____

_____

_____

_____

_____

_____

_____

_____

_____

_____

_____

_____

_____

_____

_____

_____

_____

_____

CHAPTER NINE

Free from Perfectionism

I once heard a guy talking about how surfers are constantly in search of the perfect wave. The perfect wave, he said, has the right amount of curl, a perfect tube, just at the right height for the surfer. The wave isn't so fast that you can't do tricks, but it's fast enough to make the surfer look good. The reef below is formed so that the wave breaks over it, but the reef is far enough down that if you wipe out, you don't get slammed into the coral.

He talked about how surfers travel all around the world—to Fiji, Mexico, Hawaii, and Australia—searching for the perfect wave. It's out there somewhere, they believe, but the perfect wave is elusive. No one has found it yet.

In life, so many people are in search of perfection. They want the perfect job, the perfect relationship, the perfect family, and the perfect children. People will spend thousands of dollars and go through all kinds of hoops and hurdles to obtain perfection, whether it's the perfect smile, the perfect look, or the perfect body.

I hate to dispel any illusions you might have about yourself, but you aren't perfect! The problem is, perfection is not possible. It's a target that can never be achieved. If you wait for perfect conditions, you will never get anything done. You think others have the perfect life from a distance, only to get up close and realize their lives are just as jacked up as yours.

So many people are broken because they feel they have not played the notes of life exactly right. They made a mistake, they failed at something, or they did not live up to other people's expectations of how they thought they should be. They are constantly unhappy, constantly depressed, or constantly feeling inadequate. They may look happy on the outside, but internally they are empty because to them, their life has been a failure. These people suffer from the disease of perfectionism as a method of control.

It's a very rigid view of life that refuses to accept any standard short of perfection. While it masks itself as a pursuit of success and excellence, it is really a pursuit to hide one's flaws. This leads you on a fast track toward unhappiness and depression, because perfection is an illusion, an impossibility.

The freedom to be imperfect is in line with what the apostle Paul was telling the Galatians when he wrote, "For freedom Christ has set us free. Stand firm, therefore, and do not submit again to a yoke of slavery" (Galatians 5:1 NRSV).

Paul wanted them to know that their freedom in Christ was because of the love of God and did not come from meticulously following the law. Their salvation had nothing to do with them or some idea of moral perfection, but it had everything to do with what Jesus did on Calvary's cross. As a result, they were free to live their lives without being obsessed about whether they made a mistake here or there—because salvation was by faith, and not based upon a false ideal of perfection.

The Quest for Perfection

At the time when Galatians was written, Gentile converts new to the faith were being challenged by Jewish Christians who felt that in order to be saved, a true Christian of whatever background had to observe all the 613 commandments, customs, and ritual laws in the Old Testament. And these sanctimonious saints went around monitoring people's behavior; they were like the morality police trying to determine if their moral lives were perfect.

The new converts tried to do it all. They tried to follow every command, every custom, and every prescription, but it was unrealistic and placed an impossible burden on people's heads.

This is why Paul wrote in Ephesians, "It is by grace you have been saved, through faith—and this is not from yourselves, it is the gift of God" (Ephesians 2:8 NIV). According to the gospel that Paul preached, you are saved because of God's intervention, not by your own efforts. That means you have freedom in Jesus Christ instead of being under the weight of Old Testament law. God's expectation is not that you have it all together, not that you dot every moral *i* and cross every ethical *t*, but rather that you are genuine, sincere, and committed. Therefore, you ought to be compassionate toward others whenever they miss the mark, and you ought to be compassionate toward yourself in the same way. However, I know that is sometimes easier said than done, because of how we are conditioned as children.

According to some therapists, perfectionism is learned very early in life if a child feels they are valued mainly for their achievements. The child wants to bond emotionally with their parents. They want love, affection, a hug, a kiss, and conversation. Though the parents are good people, they are not emotionally available, so when the child wants a hug or some sort of affection, the parents don't know how to connect with the child in that way.

But when the child performs well, that's when he or she gets the parents' attention. It's only when the child makes A's that the parents validate the child; it's only when they are getting an award at school and the parent sends all the family members a copy of the school program; it's only when the child is starting on the football team, the band, or the cheering squad. Then the parents go out of their way to acknowledge their child's efforts.

Yet, when the child has had a rough day at school and just wants some love, or wants to talk about feelings, the parents don't know how, so they just tell the child to go to his or her room and do homework, or to go outside and practice. That child grows up and associates his or her value with accomplishments or achievements. More dangerously, that person starts to seek the approval of other people to validate them and give them a sense of self-worth.

The problem is, since perfection is an illusion, they never quite meet the mark. When they don't perform well, when they don't pass the test, when they don't get the job, or when the relationship ends, it leaves them sad, empty, depressed, and anxious, because in their minds, it's not just that they failed at something. They feel as if *they* are a failure.

If you have ever felt that way, know that God doesn't expect you to be perfect. Only God is perfect, and perfectionism amounts to nothing more than idolatry, because you're not focusing on God but on yourself.

Good Enough Is Good Enough

Idolatry is the pursuit of something in the flesh that can only be found in or accomplished by God. Now, don't get me wrong. I'm not saying you shouldn't strive to do the best you can; you should. But you should acknowledge that even your best is marred by errors.

As highlighted in Chapter Three, the Bible says: "For all have sinned and fall short of the glory of God" (Romans 3:23 KJV). Those seeking perfection never feel a sense of fulfillment and satisfaction. Many end up addicted, depressed, and with low self-esteem because they are seeking an impossible goal.

President John Quincy Adams held more government offices than anyone else in the history of the U.S. He served with distinction as president, senator, congressman, and minister to major European powers, and participated in various capacities in the American Revolution, the War of 1812, and events leading to the Civil War. Yet at age 70, with much of that behind him, he wrote, "My whole life has been a succession of disappointments. I can scarcely recollect a single instance of success to anything that I ever undertook."[42]

Perfectionists attach their self-esteem to how they perform, and they need other people's validation to compensate for their own sense of shame, judgment, and blame. But perfection is not a requirement for you to be used by God. According to Paul, "Not that we are adequate in ourselves to consider anything as *coming* from ourselves, but our adequacy is from God" (2 Corinthians 3:5 NASB). God uses flawed people for His perfect will. The Bible does not try to cover up the fact that Abraham was a liar, Noah was a drunk, or David was an adulterer and a murderer. Yet in the church, we sometimes act as if God exclusively uses those without defects.

God's willingness to use flawed people is something you should celebrate, because it means that there's a place for you in His plan! All of us have something in our lives that God is still working out. All of us have stains on our spiritual resumés, and yet He still uses us.

That's good news in a world addicted to false idols and ideals of perfection. In fact, according to Mondovo, *photoshop* is one of the most searched words on Google every day.[43] People feel they need to edit their pictures to make it look like they have the perfect eyes, the perfect body, and the perfect life, but they are just as flawed as you and me.

We must get to the point where we accept people as they are, and we must also accept ourselves the way we are. We have to stop looking down upon and judging those who do not meet our notions of beauty, intellect, and success, because all of us are a part of the fraternity of imperfection. Your neighbor may appear to have it all together, but they don't. They may even give you the impression that their family, their finances, and their faith are unflawed, but they're not.

Paul in Galatians 5 said he wants us to be freed from the idol of perfection because the quest to always get it right, to always present the best version of yourself, imprisons you; it puts you in bondage to an impossible dream. The goal in this life is to do better, not attain perfection. In other words, you don't have to build your life on the shaky eggshell of flawlessness.

Perhaps you have heard this statement: "If you can't do it right, don't do it at all." That sounds good, but it's deeply destructive to the human spirit because it prevents people from getting to the point where they can say, "This is good enough," or, "I've done a good job, the best I could."

All of us should aim to be a better version of ourselves, but we must equally be compassionate with ourselves in the process. None of us got where we are without making some mistakes and having some personal inadequacies. You must never become so preoccupied with perfecting your life that you neglect to live your life.

Living Free

Have you ever gone on a group trip with friends or family? There's always someone who has to micromanage every detail of the trip. And sometimes, you're more stressed after the trip than you were before, because of that one person who can't enjoy the journey since they're too busy obsessing over the details.

I decided not long ago that life is not supposed to be lived like that, so I'm not going to let other people stress me out. I'm not going to allow other people to cause me to obsess about things that aren't worth obsessing over. I'm just going to enjoy the trip.

Don't be so uptight that you can't enjoy the morning sun, the sunset, or the sound of the birds. Don't be so uptight that you can't enjoy the ups and downs, the twists and turns, and the things in life that you can't anticipate. Paul said the way we enjoy the journey is to realize that in Christ we have been made free and that's enough. You don't have to impress anyone. You don't have to conform to anyone else's expectations for your life regarding what career you should have, whom you should marry, or whether you get married at all.

Paul's declaration in Galatians 5:1, "It is for freedom that Christ has set us free" (NIV), speaks to a central but often forgotten truth about humanity: all of us were born free, and we should live our lives free. Freedom and acceptance are not things one has to work for or get permission for; rather, they are things one simply embraces. Embrace your freedom. Every person is an independent center of value.

Paul says we are free for freedom's sake. The statement is circular, but Paul says it this way on purpose, because he wants us to know that we don't have to live by standards that don't come from God. Too many people try to negotiate their worth based on external and superficial stuff. They try to determine who they are by what they achieve, what they amass, and what they accomplish. When they don't achieve, they fall short, or their flaws are exposed, they develop a sense of unworthiness.

But Paul wanted them, and you, to know that your freedom, your right to exist and be happy, is independent of the external. "People look at the outward appearance, but the LORD looks at the heart" (1 Samuel 16:7 NIV). God grants you liberty as an expression of His love and as an expression of your worth, and that comes from within.

Your value is not diminished by life's tears and life's mud. Your value is independent of what you do, what you drive, and where you live. What you do is not who you are. I like what Paul said in Galatians 5:1: "For freedom Christ has set us free. Stand firm, therefore, and do not submit again to a yoke of slavery" (NRSV).

Your task is not to be perfect, but to be faithful, and God will take care of the rest. So rather than being so up-tight in life—worried about whether you're doing everything right, whether you've pleased your family or impressed your friends—just enjoy the journey.

The Blessing of Imperfection

Look again at Galatians 5:1. Paul understood that the antithesis of freedom in Christ was the bondage of perfectionism. He did not want them to return to the old way of thinking, which he compared to a yoke around their necks. As discussed earlier, a yoke was a wooden harness used to join two oxen together to pull a cart or a plough. It worked by restricting their movement. The yoke prevented the ox from exploring and enjoying the journey.

On the contrary, the journey with Christ is a journey of freedom and exploration in which mistakes are permitted. You don't have to be the perfect spouse, parent, employee, student, or Christian. Your aim is just to be faithful, because there's a blessing in imperfection. Paul said elsewhere that God's strength is made perfect in our weakness or our imperfections (2 Corinthians 12:9), so relax and let Him take care of it.

Whomever the Son has set free is free indeed (John 8:36). And if you're free, you ought to act like you're free. If you're free, you ought to walk like you're free. If you're free, you ought to talk like you're free. Paul was saying, don't let someone else put you in bondage to their own unrealistic expectations. They often tell you what you should do or say even when they haven't done those things themselves.

The reason perfectionists are in bondage, Paul implied, is because they are constantly comparing themselves to other people. In the first-century church, the Judaizers— the people who wanted new converts to embrace the Jewish law—emphasized the act of circumcision as a sign that one had submitted to God. Circumcision was a key part of Old Testament law, but the new converts were not Jewish. There was no need for them to follow that tradition, but it was a ritual that enabled the morality police to see whether others had conformed to their standard. By contrast, Paul wanted these new converts to reject the old system centered on law over love, rules over relationship, and conformity over compassion. It came down to a lifestyle that was about pleasing people, not pleasing God.

This kind of religious OCD—obsessive comparison disorder—was driving people crazy. They were spending all their time comparing their lives to others'. There's nothing wrong with wanting to improve and asking, in a self-focused way, "How can I do better?" But perfectionism is destructive. It is other-focused in an unhealthy way. It asks, "What will they think of me?" Trying to meet other people's expectations through comparison only causes pain.

Circumcision was typically performed on infants, but these Jewish Christians wanted Gentile Christians to undergo circumcision as adults, which would involve a great deal of pain, not just physically but psychologically. Paul says to "be free" because you're going to hurt yourself seeking the approval of other people.

Do you know how many people are in pain today trying to please and impress other people? Do you know how many people are working at jobs they don't like and living in houses they can't afford because they are worried about what other people will think of them? If other people don't like you, that's not your problem—that's their problem.

"Stand firm," Paul said. I believe that means to persist, hold fast, endure, and not let anybody or anything separate you from the love of God. What God was doing in the lives of these new Gentile believers was different than what He had done before, and it was not easy for Judaizers to understand. The new Christians had to learn to resist them. That's why Paul told the Ephesians, "Therefore take up the whole armor of God, so that you may be able to withstand on that evil day, and having done everything, to stand firm" (Ephesians 6:13 NRSV).

I know a younger preacher who grappled with this kind of comparison. He was told in the tenth grade that due to his academic challenges—ADHD and dyslexia—it would be best if he went into a trade rather than try to go to college. He recalls his mother, with tears running down her face, saying that he would stay on a college track even if he had to struggle through it. He was accepted at Morehouse and in due course completed the requirements for graduation to the glory of God.

However, he fell into the trap of comparing his accomplishment with those of his friends. They were going to Harvard, Princeton, Vanderbilt, and the University of Chicago after graduation, and he was struggling to get into a graduate program.

He remained upset until he was walking out of the processional after graduation, when he looked over and saw his mother, who was in the audience. She was shouting and cheering with tears running down her face. And it was then he realized that he might not have been going to Harvard or Yale for graduate school, and he might not be a Rhodes Scholar, but God had been good to him. He had come a long way and had no need to compare his achievement with that of anyone else.

There is enough bad in the best of us, and enough good in the worst of us, that we should view ourselves and each other with compassion and tolerance. You are free in Christ to be as God made you. You may not be perfect to others, but you are perfect to Him.

WORKBOOK

Chapter Nine Questions

Question: Have there been times when you were motivated by what other people thought of you? Have you felt inadequate or inferior in any way to those around you?

_____

_____

_____

_____

_____

_____

_____

_____

_____

_____

Question: Our society is obsessed with presenting ourselves as being perfect and having the perfect lifestyle, family, job, and possessions. In what ways have you felt the desire to be perfect?

_____

_____

_____

_____

_____

_____

_____

_____

_____

_____

Question: How do you deal with your mistakes? Do you secretly equate failing with failure? What can you do to learn to view mistakes as opportunities for growth?

_____

_____

_____

_____

_____

_____

_____

_____

_____

_____

_____

Action: Paul tells us that we have freedom in Christ and must not allow ourselves to be imprisoned by a yoke of slavery. In the first-century church, the big question was over circumcision for Gentile converts. What "yoke of slavery" are you facing, and what actions will you take to stand firm in your freedom?

Chapter Nine Notes

CHAPTER TEN

I'm Writing Another Chapter

"God grant me the serenity to accept the things I cannot change, courage to change the things I can, and wisdom to know the difference." The original version of the Serenity Prayer was penned by the American theologian Reinhold Niebuhr.[44] These words have been popularized by twelve-step programs, self-help gurus, and counselors alike. It is a plea for the inner willpower to surrender to God by realizing there are some situations you have no power to change, finding the strength to change the things in life that you can change, and learning how to discern the difference.

The truth is, you cannot change your pain-filled past. You can only learn from it and move on. So, how do you do that in a healthy way, without letting the past destroy your future?

Many of us must come to terms with things in our past that are painful, traumatic, and disappointing. And quite often, what helps us to move forward is being able to get closure from the people who caused so much hurt and harm in our lives.

Closure is critical because as humans, we understand the world through stories. We create a past, present, and future in our minds, and we navigate our world by structuring the events of our lives based upon this cognitive understanding. For better or for worse, we get a good sense of who we are, how we should feel, and how we are going to function from day to day when the aspects of our life story are clear and known to us.

To do that, we need answers. We want to know why a relationship ended, how someone we trusted could betray our trust and abuse us, cheat on us, and lie to us. We want to know why a parent we loved did not show us the kind of love we think we deserved as a child.

Understanding what happened helps you to reconfigure your life in a way that allows you to move forward. Not that you like what happened, or why they did it, but at least you have an explanation or an understanding so the issue can be resolved in your mind. Yet there are times when, despite your best efforts, you will be unable to get closure from the things that didn't go well in your past. Maybe the person who mistreated you died before you were able to get an explanation, or the person who fired you relocated before they told you why you didn't get the job of your dreams. Now you are stuck, unable to move into your future because of something unresolved in your past.

Having to come to terms with the fact that something you once counted on is now over can be hard. There are people today who are so stuck and trapped by the pain of their past that they can't move forward to embrace what God is trying to do in their lives right now. You can give back your ex's stuff, delete them from social media, and try to spend less time with your mutual friends. But if it's been years since a relationship ended and you're still hurting, you may need to take other steps. If you're an adult who continues to suffer from the events of your childhood, if hurtful comments or rejection from others haunt you continually, or if you can't move on from a setback that happened years ago, you need help.

Confusion to Confidence

For in the hand of the LORD there is a cup with foaming wine, well mixed; he will pour a draught from it, and all the wicked of the earth shall drain it down to the dregs. But I will rejoice forever; I will sing praises to the God of Jacob.

All the horns of the wicked I will cut off, but the horns of the righteous shall be exalted.
—Psalm 75:8–10 NRSV

Psalm 75 is a lesson on how to move forward even when getting closure on past events is not possible. In the previous two psalms, the psalmist was asking God for clarity on a series of issues with which he was struggling. He wanted to know why it seemed as if the wicked were always prospering and those who were living right were always struggling. He didn't understand why the righteous were suffering while the wicked seemed to be doing well.

And it did not seem that the psalmist got a good, clear, complete answer to all these questions. The life experiences portrayed in Psalm 73 and 74 were bad, but we see that the confusion the psalmist experienced in Psalm 73 was met with the confidence he rediscovered in Psalm 75. He was able to move on and move forward into another chapter of his life, even though he didn't get closure. That's encouraging if you have ever been imprisoned by some experience in your past.

The enemy wants you to think that the prior chapter in your life was your last chapter. But the psalmist shows us that regardless of how bad, traumatic, disappointing, and devastating our last chapter was, we can write a new chapter. He shows us how to move on when we don't get closure.

Refocus Your Attention

Notice what the psalmist said in the absence of clear closure and understanding: he said that "it is good to be near God" (Psalm 73:28 NIV), and in Psalm 75, he opened by saying, "Your Name is near" (Psalm 75:1 NIV). After focusing at length on his enemies, the psalmist reached a point where he stopped rehearsing what they had done to him and focused instead on what God could do for him. He realized that to move forward into his next season, his focus couldn't remain on the pain and struggle of seasons past or present.

Names in the Hebrew texts speak of one's character, so when the psalmist expressed how, in the midst of that which was uncertain, he wanted to be close to God's name, he was talking about holding fast to the certain, unchanging qualities of love and faithfulness revealed in the name of God. Proverbs 18:10 says, "The name of the LORD is a strong tower; the righteous run into it and are safe" (NRSV). Accordingly, the psalmist expressed that rather than his focus being on that which is unpredictable and doubtful, he was going to focus on that in which he could be confident: the name of the Lord. Freedom to pursue that which lies before you comes when you are able to walk forward in life without looking at that which lies behind you. Unfortunately, many people don't do that, because they are stuck looking back.

Do you remember the fate of Lot's wife in Genesis 19? Destruction was coming to the city of Sodom, but the Lord had provided a path for Lot and his family to move on. He released them to the possibility of a new day, a new season, a new future. The command was given, "Flee for your life; do not look back or stop anywhere in the Plain; flee to the hills, or else you will be consumed" (Genesis 19:17 NRSV). But while they were fleeing, Lot's wife looked back and was turned into a pillar of salt. Looking back caused her to become hardened and calcified. There are a lot of people like Lot's wife, whose attitudes have become hardened and whose spirits have become cynical, because they can't let go of what happened in the past.

If you want to write a new chapter in your life, you'll need to be able to change your focus so you can conceive of a future beyond the hurts and setbacks of the past. When you are constantly obsessing about the past, it can almost become an idol; you make that person who damaged you a little god who gets all your attention, energy, and power. But don't let another person, institution, or opportunity cloud your vision so much that it blocks you. Refocus on what matters, like the psalmist did. Rather than obsessing on what he could not know, the psalmist decided to focus his attention on what he could.

Regardless of what happened, where I'm going is greater than where I've been. What's ahead of you is greater than what's behind you. The opportunity you're going to get will be greater than the one you lost. The relationship that's waiting for you will surpass the one that just ended.

Leave It to God

As I read Psalm 75, I cannot help but notice the shift in language that the text assumes. In verse 1, like in other psalms, there is a universal appeal for praise; yet in verse 2, there is a shift to an announcement of divine judgment. God Himself spoke on behalf of those who were not able to get closure in Psalm 73. God announced in verse 2 that in due time, He will judge the arrogance of the wicked. Israel was not to fight fire with fire or try or seek revenge against those who had hurt them. Instead, they had to be poised and disciplined enough to let God handle their enemies.

Too many of us, during seasons of uncertainty, try to take matters into our own hands. We want to one-up those who tried to hurt us; we want to get back at those who did us wrong. However, sometimes the only response we should have for our enemies is silence. Silence does not mean we are weak; rather, it means we are letting the Lord be our defense and our vindication.

This was a hard lesson for Israel, and it is a hard lesson for us. It takes character, and a determined will, not to choose to harm those who have harmed you. It takes a secure person to resist needing to convince others of your side of the story. The true mark of your Christian maturity is revealed in your ability to let the Lord fight your battles.

This is neither a call to be weak nor a call to be passive in every situation. Instead, it is a call to rest in the assurance of the Lord as your divine defense. It is putting the weight of your pain in the hand of the One who can handle it. First Peter 5 tells us, "Cast all your anxiety on Him because he cares for you." (1 Peter 5:7 NIV). Whatever troubles you, God will sort it out because He loves you.

Learning to Love Yourself

Notice another shift in the psalmist's language. He said in the ninth verse of Psalm 75, "I will sing praise to the God of Jacob" (NIV). Up until this point, the psalmist had talked about the wicked, the arrogant, and the plot of his enemies, and God's response. However, in the last verse, he focused on himself.

Most of us never get the closure we need, because we are focused on others and what they have done instead of focusing on ourselves. We have become preoccupied and obsessed with who hurt us, how they hurt us, and who is still friends with them despite knowing that they hurt us; we never give any priority to self. You know you are not healed when you give 90 percent of your attention to the person who caused you harm and only 10 percent of your attention to yourself.

If you've ever been on a flight, you know that before the plane takes off, the pilot or cabin crew will say that if the flight loses cabin pressure, you are to put your oxygen mask on first, before you help those around you. The reason is that you can't help others if you run out of oxygen and collapse. Helping yourself gives you the capacity to help someone else. You must dare to give some priority to yourself as a person. It's a bold and courageous step with which many personality types struggle.

The psalmist used the phrase "as for me." He started to think about what he wanted and who he was, because healing begins when you discover that you are worthy enough to be healed. Many of us need a radical revival of self in which we divorce our sense of self-worth from other people's presence in our lives.

Confess and believe these words: "I am no longer going to allow my agency, my desire, nor my worth to be dictated by people and places in my past." Too many of us lose ourselves when we focus all our attention on others.

You must develop the capacity to love yourself. You never fully gain wisdom from what happened to you until you start to talk to you about you. It is mustering up enough courage to turn inward. Many of our relationships ended badly because most of us loved recklessly. Reckless love is when you start to love another person more than you love yourself. It is leasing somebody your oxygen and then wondering why you can't breathe. You can't be for others what you can't be to yourself.

Relationships of Reciprocity

If you want closure, invest in relationships of reciprocity. The psalmist said something fascinating: "As for me, I will declare this forever; I will sing praises to the God of Jacob" (Psalm 75:9 NIV). He did not say, "I will praise God," but specified "the God of Jacob." Jacob was one of the Jewish patriarchs, whose twelve sons went on to form the twelve tribes of Israel following God's promise to bless him and his descendants. In addition to the promise, God made provision for His people in other ways, such as by supplying them with a well from which they could draw water.

Many centuries later, Jesus sat at the same well and asked a Samaritan woman for a drink (John 4:6–7). A well is a place from which one draws water for refreshment and nourishment. When the psalmist said he would praise the God "of Jacob," I believe he was highlighting the principle of reciprocity. As I praise God, God replenishes me.

The principle of reciprocity is key, because too many of us are in one-sided relationships—relationships in which we give, give, give, and never get a return on our investment. This is not to say that all relationships should always be transactional, but productive and mature relationships have reciprocity, or give and take.

That doesn't mean both people do the exact same things; you are individuals, but mutually building up one another and contributing to the whole. Don't ever give all of yourself to any person, place, or thing that never gives anything to you. Any investment is a seed that will grow in the right conditions, but if you are the one doing all the sowing, that is not a relationship. That is an assignment, and one of the greatest lessons to learn in life is the difference between an assignment and a relationship. By choosing to focus on praising God, the one who refreshes us, the psalmist has given us a key: if it never feeds you the way you feed it, it is not a mutual relationship.

Further, some people and places are not even assignments; they are parasites. These are people and places in your life that suck the life out of you—that drain you and build their lives at your expense. So many of us are drained today because we fell in love with a leech, dated a parasite, and neglected to connect to people, places, and things that charged and refreshed us the way we did them. When you are hooked up with the wrong person, it's like putting a good battery and an old battery together in a remote control. It might work at the start, but eventually the power of the good battery will get drained by the lack of power in the old battery.

A friend of mine has a three-year-old daughter, and like all three-year-olds, she does everything she sees her grandmother do. Her grandmother loves flowers, so my friend bought the little one a plastic flower set he saw in a toy store. He did not know that his little girl would copy Gran and use whatever liquid she had to try to water the fake plant, waiting for it to flourish! He thought it was cute. However, what is cute at three is crazy at thirty.

Are you still trying to water an inauthentic and fake relationship? You know it's not real, because no matter how much you pour into it, it won't grow.

But this reciprocity goes deeper. The psalmist said, "I will praise the God of Jacob," not, "I will praise Jacob," because he wasn't looking to get from Jacob what he could only get from God. A part of mature relationships, of reciprocity, is knowing that people have limitations. Whenever you look for people, places, and things to make you happy and whole, you have made an idol out of them. People, places, and things are resources and aids to our wholeness and happiness, but God is the source. When you turn to Him, He will fuel your life.

One More Chapter

Life is like writing a book. Some chapters are phenomenal, and others sometimes leave little to be desired. We'd like to skip right over those. Yet every day adds a new page to our life story. Just when we think we've gotten to the end, we realize there's another chapter to be written.

The final chapter of the book of your life has not been written, and it doesn't end with the breakup, the abuse, the rejection, the heartache, or the letdown. Rather than waiting for someone else to give you the sense of resolution that you seek, write another chapter. If today is bad, remember that today is going to be tomorrow's past; so, change your focus and start looking forward, not back. That's what the psalmist has modeled for us. Move forward and write a new chapter.

WORKBOOK

Chapter Ten Questions

Question: Why is it so important to get closure from painful events of the past? In your experience, in what ways do they continue to impact you years later?

_____

_____

_____

_____

_____

_____

_____

_____

_____

_____

_____

Question: The psalmist switched his attention from looking at his problems to looking to God. Have you found this to be beneficial? What can hinder you from focusing on God instead of other people?

_____

_____

_____

_____

_____

_____

_____

_____

_____

_____

Question: Thinking about your relationships with partners, friends, and coworkers both now and in the past, which ones would you class as reciprocal? Which ones have been assignments instead, where you got little or no return on your emotional investment?

_____

_____

_____

_____

_____

_____

_____

_____

_____

_____

_____

_____

Action: Consider how you can move on from the negative events and relationships of the past through acceptance and refocusing your attention. What will you resolve before you can start writing another chapter in your life?

Chapter Ten Notes

_____

_____

_____

_____

_____

_____

_____

_____

_____

_____

_____

_____

_____

_____

_____

_____

_____

_____

_____

_____

_____

CONCLUSION

Keep Going

A young man was driving his grandfather someplace during a storm. As they were driving along the highway, the rain started to get heavier and heavier, to the point where it was making the young man's vision blurry. Worried about the storm, he asked his grandfather if he should pull over. His grandfather replied, "No, son, just keep driving."

It started to hail, and the young man noticed that other cars were pulling off the road. So he asked again, "Grandpa, should we pull over?"

"No," Grandad replied, "drive slowly and just keep moving." As he did, the wind started blowing, and big trucks now started pulling over.

The young man was really concerned about continuing, so he said to his grandfather, "We have to pull over now, Grandpa. Look at all the cars and trucks on the side of the road."

But his grandfather said, "Son, put your hazards on, drive slowly, but don't pull over."

As they proceeded, they discovered that once they got closer to their destination, the storm had ceased. His grandfather said to the young man, "Now, son, I want you to pull over."

Looking puzzled, the young man asked, "Why do you want me to pull over now? You didn't want me to pull over when it was raining or when it was hailing."

His grandad said, "Just pull over.... Now I want you to look back and tell me what you see." When the boy pulled over and looked back, he realized that everybody who pulled over was still stuck in the storm.

During life you will find yourself in storms. Things will happen. People will let you down. Disappointments will come your way. But when you find yourself in a storm of hurt, sadness, and pain, just keep driving and don't pull over. You can't pull over right here, because your deliverance is on the other side of this storm. Your miracle is on the other side of this conflict. Your healing is on the other side of this tragedy.

We don't always admit it in the moment, but when we take inventory of our lives, oftentimes we see that it wasn't the good times but the things we thought we never would have survived that made us who we are today. The apostle Paul said it was his difficulties that actually helped in the furtherance of the gospel. If he hadn't been imprisoned, for example, he wouldn't have written to the churches; his letters have given all subsequent generations the foundational teaching we need on Christian living. No wonder he would later write that "all things work together for the good for those who love God, who are called according to his purpose" (Romans 8:28 NRSV).

The psalmist may not have seen it in Psalms 73 or 74, but he realized in Psalm 75 that his pain was necessary for his promotion; that his struggles made him stronger; that his trials made him better; that his valleys positioned him for victory.

Maybe today you have a broken spirit, damaged because of the pain of the past. But don't get bitter; resolve to become better. Don't let a letdown get you down. Allow it to become motivation for your elevation. Don't let a breakup hinder you from building a future. You'll be better after this.

In the introduction to this book, we talked about the gigantic coast redwood trees and how they can grow to over three hundred feet. But what you may not know is that fire is rarely able to kill these mature redwoods. Why? Because these trees have an armor around them that protects them from being burned.

On your spiritual journey, in order to mature in your faith, you too must put on the full armor of God:

Stand firm then, with the belt of truth buckled around your waist, with the breastplate of righteousness in place, and with your feet fitted with the readiness that comes from the gospel of peace. In addition to all this, take up the shield of faith, with which you can extinguish all the flaming arrows of the evil one. Take the helmet of salvation and the sword of the Spirit, which is the word of God
—Ephesians 6: 13–17 *(NIV)*

God will guide you through the fire. He will protect you when the storms of life challenge you. Just stay in His will and don't give up, regardless of what life throws your way.

No matter what happened in your yesterday, your tomorrow will be greater. Stay focused, move forward, and seize the day. Remember that there are no limits to what you can do with God as the navigator of your life.

About the Author

Rev. Delman Coates is a graduate of Morehouse College (B.A. in Religion, 1995), Harvard Divinity School (Master of Divinity, 1998), and Columbia University (Master of Philosophy in Religion, 2002; Ph.D. in New Testament & Early Christianity, 2006). Since February 2004, Dr. Coates has served as the Senior Pastor of Mt. Ennon Baptist Church in Clinton, MD, shepherding a congregation of 10,000 members.

Dr. Coates founded the Our Money Campaign (ourmoneyus.org), an economic justice campaign that seeks to solve some of our nation's greatest social and economic challenges. He also founded the Black Church Center for Justice and Equality (theblackchurch.net) to address the social and spiritual challenges of the African American faith community. His latest project launch is No Limits with Pastor Delman (delmancoates.org), a broadcast ministry created to help strengthen, encourage, and empower people to feel God's love and live life with *no limits*.

Coates is a board member of the National Action Network. He is also a member of the Society of Biblical Literature, the Morehouse College Board of Preachers, and the NAACP. The American Civil Liberties Union (ACLU) honored Dr. Coates in 2013 for his commitment to advancing civil rights and liberties for all. The same year, *Ebony* magazine selected him as one of their "Power 100."

Dr. Coates' ministry, messages, and social activism span a variety of media platforms. He has appeared on, and been profiled in, national media such as MSNBC, WJLA (DC), CNN, Fox News, Fox Soul, *Essence* magazine, NPR, VH1, *The New York Times*, *The Washington Post*, and *Huffington Post*, and is featured in the documentary *The New Black*.

Dr. Coates is the proud father of four children: sons Nathaniel and Joshua and twin daughters Ava Marie and Leah Blair.

REFERENCES

Notes

1. Guinness World Records Ltd. "Tallest Tree Living." https://www.guinnessworldrecords.com/world-records/tallest-tree-living/.

2. Thurman, Howard. *Deep Is the Hunger.* Harper & Row, 1964.

3. Seifert, Charles C. *The Negros's or Ethiopian's Contribution to Art.* Black Classic Press, 1983, p. 5.

4. Bourne, St. Clair. *John Henrik Clarke: A Great and Mighty Walk.* Black Dot Media, 1996.

5. Kierkegaard, Soren. *Papers and Journals.* Penguin Books, 2015.

6. BBC. "The Teaching of Jesus." Bitesize. 2021, p. 3. https://www.bbc.co.uk/bitesize/guides/zkw2vk7/revision/3#:~:text=Tax%20collectors%20were%20hated%20in,foreigners%20who%20ruled%20over%20them.

7. Wiersbe, Warren W. *Be Courageous (Luke 14–24): Take Heart from Christ's Example.* David C Cook, 2010, p. 86.

8. Cobbs Leonard, Tasha. "You Know My Name." Track 7 on *Heart. Passion. Pursuit.* Motown Gospel (EGS), 2017.

9. History.com. "Tutankhamen." November 9, 2009. Updated July 20, 2020. https://www.history.com/topics/ancient-history/tutankhamen.

10. Powell, Mark Allan. *Supplement to* Introducing the New Testament. 2nd edition. Baker Academic, 2018, p. 1770. http://cdn.bakerpublishinggroup.com/processed/esource-assets/files/2920/original/Powell_Explore_readings_all.pdf.

11. Bradshaw, John. *Healing the Shame That Binds You*. Health Communications, 1988, p. 18.

12. Hamer, Fannie Lou, and Davis W. Houck. *The Speeches of Fannie Lou Hamer: To Tell It Like It Is*. University Press of Mississippi, 2011, p. 62.

13. Buck, Chris, and Jennifer Lee, dir. *Frozen*. Walt Disney Studios Motions Pictures, 2013.

14. Korzybski, Alfred, and Russell Meyers. *Science and Sanity; an Introduction to Non-Aristotelian Systems and General Semantics*. International Non-Aristotelian Library Publishing Company, 1958, p. 37.

15. The Greater Good Science Center at the University of California, Berkeley. "What Is Forgiveness?" Greater Good Magazine. 2021. https://greatergood.berkeley.edu/topic/forgiveness/definition#:~:text=Psychologists%20generally%20define%20forgiveness%20as,they%20actually%20deserve%20your%20forgiveness.

16. Aram, Stephen. "Releasing Control." Sermon Central. November 14, 2019. https://www.sermoncentral.com/sermons/releasing-control-stephen-aram-sermon-on-control-243512?ref=SermonSerps.

17. Watkinson, William Lonsdale. *The Supreme Conquest: And Other Sermons Preached in America*. F. H. Revell Company, 1907, p. 218.

18. *Bible Hub,* "self-control." https://biblehub.com/topical/s/self-control.htm.

19. Kenya CitizenTV. "Eliud Magut's Marathon Woes." YouTube video. April 29, 2014. https://www.youtube.com/watch?v=dfpO7j JTEvo&feature=emb_title.

20. *Lexico,* "yoke." https://www.lexico.com/definition/yoke.

21. Cordeiro, Wayne. *Leading on Empty: Refilling Your Tank and Renewing Your Passion.* Baker Publishing Group, 2010, p. 122. See also: Hornok, Marcia K. *Discipleship Journal* 60 (1990), p. 23.

22. Rath, Tom. *Are You Fully Charged? The 3 Keys to Energizing Your Work and Life.* Missionday, 2015.

23. Jelks, Randal Maurice. *Benjamin Elijah Mays, Schoolmaster of the Movement: A Biography.* University of North Carolina Press, 2012, p. 189.

24. Groeschel, Craig. *It: How Churches and Leaders Can Get It and Keep It.* Zondervan, 2008.

25. Dictionary.com, "slang." https://www.dictionary.com/e/slang/do-you/.

26. Cordeiro, Wayne. *Leading on Empty,* p. 79.

27. *Thayer's Greek Lexicon,* "Strongs NT 266." In *Blue Letter Bible,* "Strong's G266 – hamartia." https://www.blueletterbible.org/lang/lexicon/lexicon.cfm?Strongs=G266&t=KJV.

28. *Encyclopaedia Britannica,* "carpe diem." https://www.britannica.com/topic/carpe-diem.

29. *Encyclopaedia Britannica,* "carpe diem."

30. Mother Teresa. *A Simple Path.* Random House Publishing Group, 2007, p. 74.

31. Emerson, Ralph Waldo. *Prose Works of Ralph Waldo Emerson.*

Houghton, Mifflin, 1880, p. 100.

32. Donald Lawrence. "Encourage Yourself." Track 2 on *Finalé Act II*. EMI Gospel (EGS), 2006.

33. Felix, Chebem, and Ifeanyi Egerue. *Lessons About Life, Love, Hate and Human Experience*. AuthorHouse, 2008, p. 30.

34. Benioff, David, and D. B. Weiss. *Game of Thrones*. Warner Bros. Television Distribution, 2011–2019.

35. Hugo, Victor. *Things Seen*. Harper & Brothers, 1887, p. 63.

36. Elffers, Joost, and Robert Greene. *The 48 Laws of Power*. Penguin Publishing Group, 2000.

37. Forde, Pat. "Offense Wins Championships: College Football Playoff Proves Scoring Has Supplanted Defense as a Way to Win It All." January 2, 2019. https://www.yahoo.com/lifestyle/offense-wins-championships-college-football-playoff-proves-scoring-supplanted-defense-way-win-024235818.html.

38. NBA.com Staff. "Top Moments: Pistons Shock NBA World, Win Championship in 2004." NBA.com. August 24, 2017. https://www.nba.com/history/top-moments/2004-pistons-championship.

39. Cleveland, James. "Victory Shall Be Mine." Track 12 on *A Tribute to the King*, Malaco Records, 1991.

40. Trotter, William Finlayson, and Blaise Pascal. *Pensees*. E. P. Dutton, 1958.

41. King, Martin Luther, Jr. "Remaining Awake Through a Great Revolution." Delivered at the National Cathedral, Washington, D.C., on March 31, 1968. *Congressional Record*. April 9, 1968. The Martin Luther King, Jr. Research and Education Institute. https://kinginstitute.stanford.edu/king-papers/publications/knock-

midnight-inspiration-great-sermons-reverend-martin-luther-king-jr-10.

42. Adams, John Quincy, and Charles Francis Adams. *Memoirs of John Quincy Adams: Comprising Portions of His Diary from 1795 to 1848.* Vol. 9. J. B. Lippincott & Company, 1874, p. 14.

43. Mondovo. "The Most Searched Words on Google." https://www.mondovo.com/keywords/most-searched-words-on-google.

44. Alcoholics Anonymous. "Origin of the Serenity Prayer: A Historical Paper." https://www.aa.org/assets/en_US/smf-129_en.pdf.